Textured
Canvas Work

MILNER CRAFT SERIES

Textured Canvas Work

ALISON PARK

SALLY MILNER PUBLISHING

First published in 1994 by
Sally Milner Publishing Pty Ltd
558 Darling Street
Rozelle NSW 2039 Australia

© Alison Park 1994

Design concept by David Constable
Design layout by Gatya Kelly, Doric Order
Photography by Benjamin Huie
Typeset in Australia by Asset Typesetting Pty Ltd
Printed in Australia by Pirie Printing Pty Ltd

National Library of Australia Cataloguing-in-Publication data:

Park, Alison.
    Textured canvas work.

    ISBN 1 86351 132 6.

    1. Canvas embroidery. 2. Canvas embroidery — Patterns.
    I. Title.

746.442

CONTENTS

INTRODUCTION

When I first started stitching on canvas I felt that only the traditional canvas-work stitches could be used. I was constantly frustrated, as I love texture and sculptural effects, while the majority of stitches I found in books were smooth or low relief. To obtain texture and depth in my work, I turned to other techniques such as quilted appliqué, crochet and knitting. Then I discovered surface stitchery and a door opened for me. Combining surface stitchery with traditional stitches allows me to achieve the visual depth that I love. In fact, I use any stitchery, thread or technique that will allow me to get the effect that I am after.

In this book the projects, eight small scenes, cover some of the stitches and threads that I use to achieve dimension and texture. I hope by the time you have worked all or some of these, you will have gained enough confidence to experiment on your next canvas.

MATERIALS AND EQUIPMENT

MATERIALS

Y ou have decided to take the plunge and move on from printed needlepoint or long-stitch designs and stitch your own design on bare canvas. You now have to make some choices as to the size and type of canvas and the threads you will use.

CANVAS

There are two main types of canvas weave available — single and double thread — and a variety of different mesh sizes and colours.

Single Thread

This is also called 'mono' canvas. Single thread canvas is available in two types of weave — regular and interlock — and both come in various mesh sizes.

- Regular canvas has an ordinary weave of warp or vertical threads and weft or horizontal threads and, on closer inspection of the canvas, you will see the threads weaving under and over. It is available in white, ecru or yellow. This canvas has some give in it and is, therefore, useful for furnishing articles and pulled work. You must remember to bind the edges, as it will fray.
- Interlock canvas, you will see, if you look closely at the intersections of the warp and weft threads, has either the warp threads splitting the weft threads or two weft threads wrapped around the warp thread. This canvas is the type predominately used in long-stitch kits. It is available in white only. The interlocking prevents the movement or unravelling of threads, so the edges may be trimmed close to the stitching and binding is not necessary.

Double Thread

This is also called 'penelope canvas' and has two threads running in both directions. It is available in ecru, white or brown. When stitching double canvas, you usually work over two threads. If you want to stitch fine details you work over a single thread; this is known as 'petit point'. The majority of canvases that you can purchase with a printed design use double thread canvas as it allows the embroiderer to work fine details in the middle of normal stitching with comparative ease. It is not available in very fine mesh sizes.

Mesh Sizing

When purchasing canvas, such an array of mesh sizes is available that the task of choosing is quite daunting. It is important that you understand mesh size as it has a bearing on the finished size of your design and it will also affect the thickness of the threads you select, the stitches you use and size of needle required.

Mesh size is the number of warp threads to one linear inch (2.5 cm), and is listed in design books as, for example, '12-count mesh'. If a design calls for a definite number of threads to be stitched over, count the threads, as accuracy is not guaranteed by a tape measure.

If you are working a design from a graph, the finished size will be altered by using a different size mesh to the one specified in the project. If you decide to use a different mesh size, remember that the thickness of threads may have to be altered as well.

Working out the finished size of a graphed design according to the various mesh sizes is quite a simple task. Divide the number of graph squares by the mesh size. For example, a graph design of 120 squares across and 120 squares down when worked on 10-count mesh will measure 30 cm x 30 cm (12 in x 12 in), and when worked on 12-count mesh will measure 25 cm x 25 cm (10 in x 10 in).

Below is a list of canvas sizes commonly available.

- Rug canvas in 3- and 4-count.
- Double canvas in 8- to 14-count.
- Single canvas in 10- to 16-count.
- Single canvas in 18- to 22-count is used for petit point.
- Silk gauze in counts of 32 and upwards is also used for petit point (the background area can be left unstitched if desired).

THREADS

In the past it was usual for only wool or stranded cotton to be used, with the whole design worked in the same thread. With the wide variety of threads available today you are not limited to a single type of thread, but can choose the one to suit the visual effect you wish to portray. I have listed the threads used in the projects, but you may wish to substitute others to suit your own individual taste.

Wool

The wool yarns designed especially for canvas work are as follows.

- Tapestry is a 4-ply wool available in a large range of colours.
- Persian is a three-stranded 2-ply wool; you can separate the strands, which allows you to adjust the thickness to obtain the correct coverage of the canvas. This yarn is known by other names, depending on the manufacturer.
- Crewel is a lightly twisted 2-ply wool that comes in a range of soft colours.
- Medici is a very fine 1-ply wool that is manufactured by DMC for use in petit point, but it is lovely to work with in other areas as well.

Cotton

Below are some of the cotton embroidery threads that can be used to effect in canvas work.

- Stranded consists of six strands of soft, loosely twisted mercerised cotton. It can be separated into individual strands, allowing you to use the strands singly or in any number to ensure coverage of the canvas. It is also known as 'floss'.
- Coton retors mat is a soft, twisted, 5-ply thread with a matt finish, which cannot be divided. It is also known as 'soft embroidery cotton'.
- Perle coton is a shiny, twisted, 2-ply thread available in a wide range of colours and thicknesses. This thread cannot be divided. When selecting the thread, No. 3 is the thickest, while No. 5 is finer and has the largest range of colours. You can obtain finer perle coton (look for higher numbers), but the colour range is often limited in the finer threads.
- Flower is a fine, twisted thread made by DMC. It has a slight sheen and you will need multiple threads to cover the canvas.
- Dansk Fleur is a matt, 5-strand cotton: one strand of Dansk Fleur is equivalent to two strands of stranded cotton. It is also known as 'Danish flower' thread.

Other Threads

There are many other threads that can be used for canvas work; below are just some that I have used.

- Marlitt is a brand name for a viscose and rayon stranded thread. It has high lustre and is very slippery to work with, so use shorter lengths when stitching with this thread.

- Madeira is another brand name for a thread that does not have as high a lustre as Marlitt, but is very similar to work with.
- Silk threads are available in a wide range of twists, strands and lustres. Make your selection depending on the effect you wish to achieve.
- A vast array of hand or overdyed yarns is now available, including wool, perle coton and stranded cotton, and the colour combinations within an individual skein present a visual feast. Many of the overdyed yarns are produced by individual artisans, so colour combinations cannot be relied on from one dye batch to the next. Some thread manufacturers, seeing the market potential, are also selling these threads and, due to their processing, the colour variations are not as extreme. When purchasing this type of thread, ensure that you buy enough of the batch to complete the project, to avoid disappointment. Using these threads can actually help you to change colours at random within a stitch pattern, and give your work a very natural look.
- Ordinary knitting yarns can be used. The variety available is wide; try not just the pure wools, but a combination of fibres. Some of the yarns that are used for details or highlights in garments are quite suitable for canvas work, although the finer yarns are the easiest to work with. In fact, the combinations of different fibre in the one yarn can make life that little bit easier when stitching — and the visual effect can be quite stunning.

EQUIPMENT

NEEDLES

Tapestry needles have large eyes, are short in length and have blunt tips. They are available in different sizes, with the length becoming shorter as the eye decreases in size. Needles can be bought in packets of mixed sizes (the most commonly included are sizes 18–22) or packets with a single size of needles.

The size of needle you need will depend on the mesh size of your canvas. To select the correct size, drop the needle diagonally into a hole in your canvas. The eye should stop the needle from dropping straight through, but as you pull the needle through, the canvas threads should not be distorted.

FRAMES

You must use a frame if you wish to produce clean, even stitches with a minimum of distortion to the finished canvas. A frame also allows you to couch threads and appliqué extra canvas pieces with relative ease.

The best frame to use is rectangular, with the side pieces long enough to allow a large area of the design to be seen (for large canvases, 34 cm [14 in] between the dowels is a good length). The tape on the dowels at the top and bottom should be the full width of the canvas (the design area, plus edge allowances). **Do not** have your dowels too long or your frame will be uncomfortable to use; or too short, so that you have to fold over the sides of the canvas.

FRAME STANDS

Some people like to have their frame supported by a stand, leaving them free to work with both hands. The resulting stitching is more flowing and has an even tension.

There are two types of stands: table and floor. The table stand has short legs, and you should check that when sitting at the table you are level with the frame. The best floor stand is one where the height of the frame can be adjusted to the height of your chair. Some stands also have moveable arms that allow the frame to be angled to a comfortable position for stitching.

SCISSORS

You will need two pairs of scissors.

- Large scissors for cutting paper or canvas. Do not use your good dressmaking scissors as canvas is a harsh material that will quickly blunt them.
- Small scissors with a sharp point for embroidery. These must always be kept sharp to ensure threads are cut cleanly.

THIMBLE

The use of a thimble is a matter of personal preference.

MARKING PEN

This is used to draw the design on the canvas. A water-erasable pen is useful as mistakes can be washed off, but be careful not to press too heavily. Other felt-tipped pens can be used, but check on a spare piece of canvas to see if the colour runs before working on your actual design. Never choose a dark colour as it may show through your stitching.

BINDING TAPE

Canvas is a harsh material, so the edges must be bound before it is attached to the frame. You can use either of the following:

- Masking tape, as used for household painting, is adequate, but make sure that the brand you choose will adhere to the canvas.
- Material tape can easily be sewn to the canvas by hand or machine.

PREPARATION

On having decided not to use a purchased canvas, you may feel bewildered and uncertain where to begin, but preparation is the key to success. There are many stages prior to stitching, but the time spent on design, selecting the type and mesh size for your canvas, preparing the canvas and choosing the threads is well worth the effort and will allow you to get a real sense of personal achievement at the end.

DESIGN

Where do you begin when designing a scene? A simple starting point is to choose a favourite scene from a holiday snap, book or magazine. The entire picture need not be used; you can choose a pleasing portion of the scene. Experiment with a slide mount or a paper frame to find the part that will make the most effective picture.

TRANSFERRING THE DESIGN TO PAPER

Using clear tracing paper and a soft B-leaded pencil, draw the border on the paper. Then trace the outline of the main features of the photograph within the border. Include only such things as buildings, doors, windows, trees and shrubs at this stage; do not worry about the fine details, such as individual window panes. When you are happy with the outlines on the tracing paper, go over the pencil lines with a black felt-tipped pen. If the finished size of the piece is to be larger than the tracing, take the drawing along to your local copy shop to have it enlarged by photocopier.

CANVAS

The type, colour and mesh size of the canvas is your next decision. What you must keep in mind is the threads, stitches and colours that you intend to work with. If you will be using a large proportion of dark colours, then try to purchase an ecru canvas, as a white canvas may show through where the threads do not give full coverage. Only choose double thread canvas if you are planning to have fine details in among your normal stitching. If you do choose this, remember that it does limit the stitches and threads you can use to some extent.

For all the projects in this book I used single-thread interlock 14-count canvas. The reasons for this choice are threefold.

1. The canvas threads are interlocked and will not move when stitched by a beginner.
2. Very few of the threads used in the project have required adjustments to the number of strands used.
3. There is no fine stitch detailing in any of the projects.

I used white canvas as it is the colour most readily available in shops for this type and mesh size.

Once you have decided on the canvas type and mesh, you now have to consider how much canvas you actually need to purchase. To calculate this, take the outside measurements of the scene and add 10 cm (4 in) to all sides. Any selvedge on the canvas **must be cut off** prior to measuring, as it will interfere with the stitching tension. You will also need an extra 20 cm x 30 cm (8 in x 12 in) piece of canvas to practise the stitches and test the thickness of threads for correct coverage before moving onto the actual canvas.

TRANSFERRING THE DESIGN TO CANVAS

1. Lay your finished design on a smooth flat surface and secure it at the corners.
2. Place your canvas over the design. Make sure that there is an even amount of canvas around the edges of the border with a minimum of 10 cm (4 in) on all sides.
3. Secure the canvas at the corners.
4. Mark the borders of the design on the canvas with a marking pen. You will find that canvas has 'channels' between the actual threads. When marking the outside edge you will find it easier to draw a straight line if you run your pen along the channels rather than along a thread, and it will give a clear edge to your stitching.
5. With your marking pen, trace the design on the canvas. Before removing the canvas, check that you have traced all the outlines.

BINDING THE CANVAS

The canvas must have all edges bound to stop the threads unravelling and prevent the rough edges catching on your embroidery threads. The two most common methods of binding are to stick on masking tape, the kind used by household painters, or sewing on bias-binding tape by machine using a zig-zag stitch. Once this is done, you are ready to mount your canvas on a working frame.

MOUNTING THE CANVAS ON A FRAME

1. Mark the centre of the top and bottom edges of your canvas.
2. Mark the centre of the tape on the top and bottom dowels of the frame. Do not extend the tape.
3. Place the top edge of the canvas between the top dowel and the tape and, matching the centre of the canvas to the centre of the tape, pin.

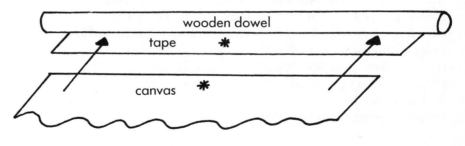

4. Stitch the canvas to the tape using a strong cotton.

5. Repeat steps 3 and 4 with the bottom edge of the canvas.

6. Position the dowels in the side pieces of the frame, making sure the canvas is square (any angling of the canvas will cause distortion) before tightening the screws.

7. To ensure the canvas is taut in the frame, but without extending or distorting the sides of the canvas, lace the side edges of the canvas to the side pieces of the frame, using a very strong thread.

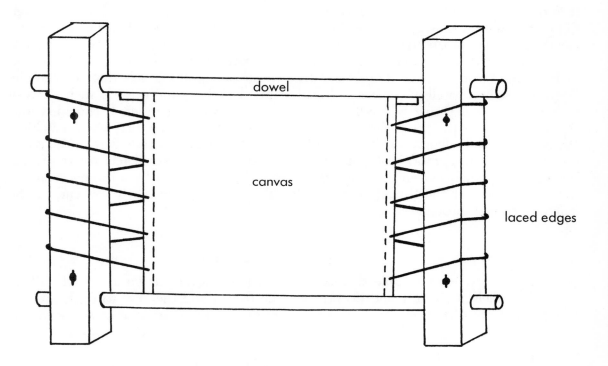

8. You will need to readjust and tighten the canvas constantly as stitching will loosen the tension.

BASIC RULES FOR STITCHING

There are many stitches that may be used to great effect on canvas, but an understanding of the basics will always stand you in good stead when experimenting. Before explaining the actual stitches, here are a few basic rules that will help you.

LENGTH OF THREAD

It is quite important that the thread is not too long, as constantly pulling it through the canvas will cause wear on the thread and will spoil the finished surface. The best length will vary depending on the type of thread and stitches you are working, but a comfortable thread is the length of your forearm. To calculate this, hold the end of the yarn between your thumb and first finger and pull enough thread from the skein to reach your elbow, cut the thread at this length. Some threads such as wool have a grain or nap that allows the fibres to lie against each other. If threaded into the needle against the grain, this will cause the thread to become furry when stitching. When you run the length of the thread between the finger and thumb with the grain, the thread will feel smooth; if you run it against the grain, it will feel rough. When threading the newly cut end through the needle check that you have the nap running the correct way. If the thread is still in the skein, thread the newly cut end of the length of thread through the needle.

THREADING A NEEDLE

Some people do have trouble threading the needle. Never cut your thread straight across but angle it slightly, and do not lick the thread and then try to push the end through the eye of the needle. If you find you have trouble, try one of the following methods.

1. Hold your needle with blunt tip out and fold a short length of the cut thread over the needle. Tighten the thread over the needle and slide it off the tip. Keeping the thread pinched, push the fold through the eye of the needle.

2. Cut a narrow strip of paper 2 cm (1 in) long. Trim the width so that it will feed through the eye of the needle smoothly. Fold the paper in half lengthwise. Place the cut end of the thread at the fold of the paper with the thread along the length of the paper. Fold the paper over to enclose the end of the thread, pinch the paper and push the folded end of the paper through the eye of the needle.

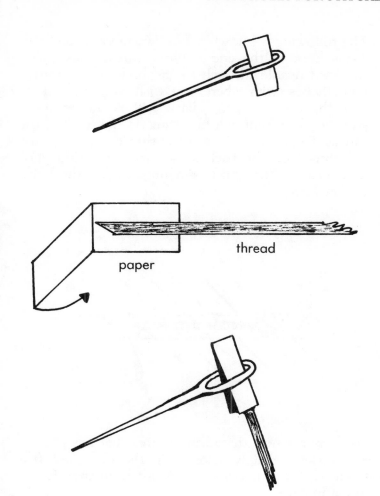

paper

thread

If you still have difficulties, then purchase a commercial needle threader.

ANCHORING A THREAD

When starting to stitch in an unworked area of canvas there are two methods of anchoring your new thread.

1. Bring your needle through the canvas to the front for the first stitch, leaving a 2 cm (1 in) length of thread at the back of the canvas. This thread should lie in the direction you are going to stitch. Work the first five stitches so that they cover the tail of thread on the back. The stitches will anchor the thread in place. Try not to split the thread at the back as you stitch.

2. The following is known as the 'waste knot' method. Tie a knot in the end of your thread. Take your threaded needle through to the back of the canvas five stitches from where you wish to start, making sure the thread on the back will lie under those stitches. Your knot will be sitting on the front of the canvas. Begin to stitch over the thread, ensuring that the thread on the back is not split as you anchor it in place. When your stitching reaches the knot, cut the knot off.

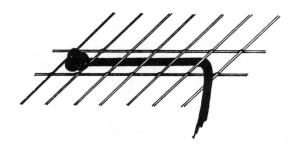

To anchor a new thread in an area that has already been worked, simply take your thread under five adjoining stitches, making a back stitch on the fifth to secure it in place.

TRADITIONAL STITCHES

There are three basic stitches traditionally used in canvas work. They appear to be the same on the front of the canvas, but how you work the stitch, the effect on the reverse side and the places they are used are quite different. You need to be familiar with all three, as each has a different purpose and uses a different amount of yarn. The stitches are half cross stitch, continental or tent stitch and basketweave or diagonal tent stitch. The name basketweave, which I prefer to use, is American in origin.

Half cross is the stitch usually taught to people by friends or shop assistants when they purchase their first canvas. However, most design books specify tent stitch in the directions, with horizontal rows worked in continental stitch and diagonal rows in basketweave, as these stitches give much better coverage of the canvas.

Many people, when taught half cross stitch and continental stitch, turn their canvas upside down to stitch the return row, this habit can cause confusion when you are working other stitches. See page 27 for instructions on how to work this stitch in both directions.

HALF CROSS

This stitch is so called because it is the first half of a cross stitch. It is only ever used on wall hangings as it gives a very poor backing. The amount of yarn used in stitching is minimal.

CONTINENTAL OR TENT

This stitch was used in early times to copy the expensive woven tapestry wall hangings. The main disadvantage with this stitch compared to other basic stitches is that it causes distortion of the canvas. It uses one and a half times the amount of yarn of half cross stitch, but does give a better stitch definition and the backing is thicker, as there is a diagonal stitch on the reverse that is longer than on the front. This stitch should be worked on a frame to minimise the distortion.

If you wish to work fine detailing on a printed canvas, this stitch is also used for petit point. Petit point is not used in the projects in this book as it can only be worked on very fine single thread canvas (18-count and higher) or on double thread canvas. You follow the stitch directions in exactly the same way on single thread canvas, but using finer threads. On double thread canvas you will split the canvas and, instead of taking your stitch over two canvas threads, you stitch over a single thread. Do remember to thin your thread in order to avoid distortion and an uneven stitch surface.

Be careful when turning at the end of one row and starting the next not to revert to a different stitch; for example, changing from half cross stitch to continental or vice versa. Work three stitches of the new row, then look at the back of the work to ensure that the stitch is correct on both sides. If you do this, any error will be picked up immediately and only three stitches will need to be unpicked, not a whole row.

BASKETWEAVE OR DIAGONAL TENT

Basketweave is the name given to this stitch, as on the back of the work it resembles the weave of a basket. Unlike half cross and continental stitches, this stitch is worked in diagonal rows. This stitch does not distort the canvas and, therefore, is used for working between other stitches. It is excellent for large areas of background or furnishings where a stitch with some give is needed to add strength to the canvas. This stitch must always be started in the top right-hand corner of the canvas.

STITCH TECHNIQUES

When you are working without the canvas in a frame there is a tendency to use continuous stitching; that is, the needle is pushed in and out of the canvas and drawn through in one movement. When the canvas is mounted in a frame it is easier to use the stab method, where the needle is taken to the back in one movement and returned to the front in another. This method is best, as it ensures a minimum of friction on your thread.

FINISHING THREADS

As you work, do not let the thread get shorter than twice the length of the needle you are using. If you allow the thread to get too short, the last stitch will be pulled too tight when you finish off. To finish a thread, turn to the wrong side of the canvas and run the thread under the last four stitches worked, then cut off the excess thread close to the stitching. For stitches with poor backings, such as half cross, it is better to weave the finishing thread under and over the last stitches worked rather than simply running under the stitches. By doing this the tension is distributed among alternate stitches rather than only on the last four, which then have a tendency to drop below the level of the other stitches.

MISTAKES

What do you do if you make a mistake? You will have to unpick the stitches; if more than three stitches have to be unpicked do not try to restitch with the same thread, but cut it off, undo the offending portion and start again.

STRIPPING THREADS

This technique is used on threads that can be separated, such as stranded cotton, and will help you to achieve the maximum coverage and effect from your threads. To do this, cut a length from the skein, separate it into individual strands, then place the strands back together. To check that the threads do cover the canvas satisfactorily, work the chosen stitch on a spare piece of canvas so that you can, if necessary, adjust the number of strands before working your design. By stripping the threads, which allows them to lie flat, a minimum amount of thread will be used to achieve the maximum effect.

COMPENSATING STITCHES

Half cross, continental and basketweave are all small stitches worked over one thread, therefore, they allow colour changes to be worked easily in small areas. However, other canvas stitches, which vary greatly in size, may be more difficult to fit into small areas and may require adjustments. Where working a full stitch would mean you extend beyond the area's outline, then it is necessary to work a partial or compensating stitch. Until you understand pattern flows, it is easier to choose a starting point within the area that allows a long pattern flow to be stitched. Work the entire area with complete stitches, leaving the compensating stitches until last. Do not be tempted to extend the full stitch to fill an area rather than work a compensating stitch and keep the stitch at the same angle as the other stitches. When you are more experienced, you may work compensating stitches with the other stitches. In the diagram on page 18, the dark lines are full stitches and the light lines are compensating stitches to fill the area.

SACRIFICE ROWS

A certain amount of the stitched area on any canvas is lost under the lip of the frame or mount board. When working with different stitches the embroiderer will have worked compensating stitches in some places, while in others textured stitches will have been worked right to the outer edge. The loss of a few rows of stitching can distort a design and textured stitches may make it impossible for the mount board to lie flat. To avoid this and offset any rows that disappear under the frame, extend the design by working two rows of half cross stitch, changing the colour and threads to match the adjacent stitching. Any movement of the framing materials or distortion of the canvas will then not be very noticeable at the edge of the piece. These extra stitches are called 'sacrifice rows'.

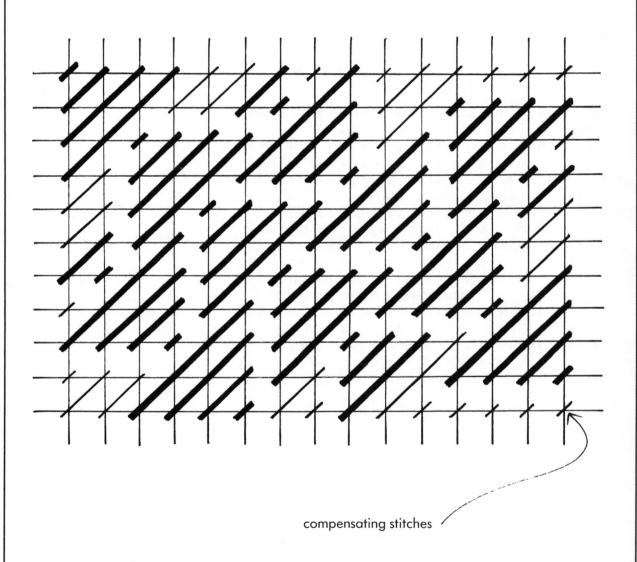

compensating stitches

Compensation

STITCHES, THREADS AND COLOUR
FOR EFFECT

How do you achieve the illusion of depth on a flat surface? With paintings the artist uses colour and perspective, while the embroiderer can use a combination of flat and textured areas, change the direction of the stitch and work with different weights of thread.

To achieve a natural effect, you must have a stitching strategy. With the projects in this book the areas are listed in order of stitching, some areas needing to be worked first. When planning your stitching, look for areas that are in the background and have objects that overlap them; for example, walls or paths with overhanging plants. These areas are usually flat and are worked first using basic canvas stitches. Textured stitches in the background area should be worked after all the canvas stitches have been completed.

Flat areas are a vital component of your design as they offset the textured stitches. They can also add life to the design, as by simply changing the stitch direction or by using different shades of thread, you can make it appear that you have turned a corner.

STITCH DIRECTION

Areas within a picture have a directional flow; these can be compared to the nap on such fabrics as velvet. When you choose a stitch pattern from a book and follow the directions correctly, but on completion still feel that something is wrong, it could be that the direction of the stitches or stitch pattern is working against the nap of the area or that the stitch pattern is too large to achieve perspective in the area. The majority of canvas stitch patterns, with only a few exceptions, can be changed to flow in the opposite direction. A little time spent working out the direction that a stitch should go is well worth the effort.

When choosing a stitch to fit into an area, remember that it is not the individual stitch that determines the directional flow but the overall stitch pattern. This can be seen with Milanese stitch, shown on page 20, where the individual stitches go from bottom left to top right but the direction of the stitch pattern flows from bottom right to top left.

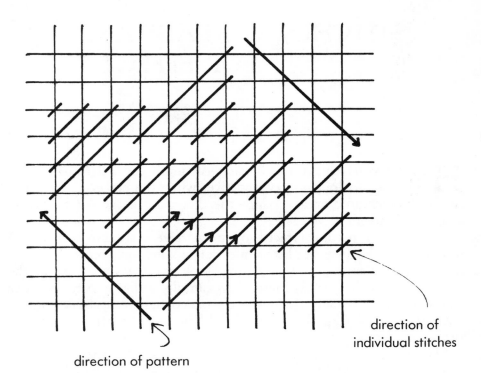

Milanese stitch showing direction of patterns and stitches

direction of pattern

direction of individual stitches

Before starting to stitch, it is necessary to determine the direction of your stitch pattern. A simple method is to make a quick pencil sketch (nothing elaborate) of the areas in question and draw diagonal lines to indicate the direction of the stitches. The direction will, to some extent, be determined by the angle at which you are looking at the scene. Are you standing directly in front, to the left or right of the scene?

COLOUR

As well as the stitch direction, colour also can enhance the feeling of depth. If an area is meant to be in the open it will have a certain amount of sunlight reflecting off it, therefore a light shade of the colour (though not necessarily a light colour) should be used. As an area recedes into shadow, use shades that darken to a corresponding depth.

Once the flat areas are completed, the textures can be added with surface stitches. As a painter would do, start with the areas in the background and work towards those in the foreground. To give as natural a feel as possible, allow the stitching to overlap into the neighbouring areas. Take time to study trees, shrubs and flowers. Close inspection of trees and shrubs will show that there are usually two or three shades: dark in the centre of the plant, a middle shade to represent the mature leaves seen on the outside, and light for the new growth. Try to reproduce these shades in your stitching as they will help to achieve a natural effect.

To obtain this effect the area is worked in three stages.

1. Using the darkest shade of the thread, work small patches of the stitch scattered from the middle to the base of the area, with an occasional stitch towards the top.
2. Change to the middle shade and stitch larger patches towards the top of the area and fill in the middle and base. Allow some of the stitches to overlap the edges of the darker stitching.
3. With the lightest shade of thread fill in the rest of the area, again overlapping the edges of the other shades, and also work the occasional stitch at the base of the area.

Unlike the majority of canvas stitches, the surface stitches must be worked at random in different directions and overlap each other to achieve a textured surface.

COMBINING STITCHES

The combination of canvas stitches and colour allows you to represent a wide range of building materials, with endless possibilities for structures such as walls.

A sandstone wall, a brick wall with mortar or a stone wall with cement render are a few of the many possibilities that can result from combining stitches.

As discussed earlier in this chapter, the direction of the flow of the stitch pattern can be changed to help give an impression of perspective, but individual stitch patterns can also be changed. A stitch pattern such as cashmere has a rectangular shape when worked in staggered rows, so it is ideal to represent a brick wall. By adding an extra stitch and surrounding with continental stitches, it becomes a brick wall with mortar. Make the diagonal stitches longer to increase the rectangle depth and vary the size of the rectangles within an area and it will resemble a sandstone wall. Of course the effect of varying the stitch pattern will not succeed visually unless you also use different threads and colours.

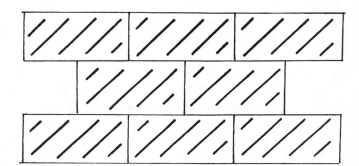

Brick wall

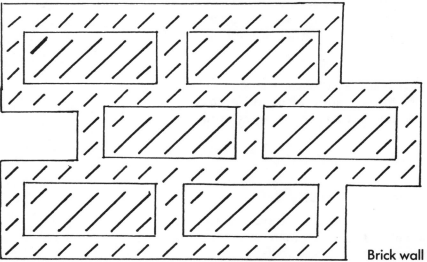

Brick wall with mortar

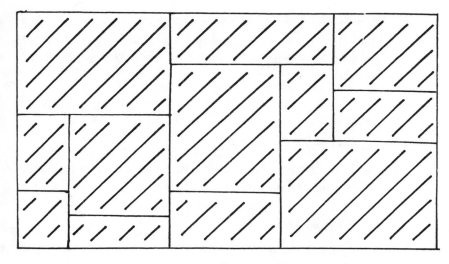

Sandstone wall

THREADS

The threads you choose will affect the impact of the scene. Sky, water, paths, roads, building materials and plants all need different thread and colour combinations to maximise their visual effect.

Matching a thread to the texture you wish to depict will enhance a stitched scene; for example, use a shiny thread to represent a window pane or high-gloss paint. Take time to look around and work out which threads could represent the different surfaces, but do not limit yourself to using one thread at a time. Very interesting effects can be achieved by working different colours, shades or types of thread together in the one needle. Another way to achieve natural depth is to combine dull and shiny threads in your work, allowing them to twist as you stitch, rather than stitching the dull thread first and then working over the top with the shiny thread.

Over the years I have found a selection of threads that I constantly use for particular effects. However, it must be remembered these threads may need to be varied when using a canvas of a different mesh size. The examples of stitch and thread effects below are merely a sample of their many possible uses. Only by experimenting with other threads and colours will new interpretations be discovered.

WOOL

Tapestry

This may be too heavy to use for the background or with canvas stitches on 14-count mesh, but it helps to bring a texture forward when used for foreground surface stitches or as a padding for other threads.

Crewel, Medici and Overdyed

These can be worked in any area or stitch, as they are lightweight wools and you can alter the number of strands.

COTTONS

Stranded and Overdyed Floss

As these threads have a sheen, they are very effective where light reflects off the surface.

Coton Retors Mat

Although a thick matt thread, this is lovely where a soft or velvety effect is required.

Perle Coton

The sheen varies depending on the thread thickness: No. 5 is shinier than No. 3. For this reason I tend to use two strands of No. 5 rather than one strand of No. 3. The twist in the thread means that the sheen is different to stranded cotton.

Dansk Fleur

A lovely, fine, matt thread. Multiple threads are needed to ensure coverage of the canvas.

WHERE TO USE THREADS

YARN	USE
Tapestry Wool	Foreground greenery; padding for greenery
Crewel, Medici and Overdyed	Bricks; flowers; grass; leaves; plants; thatch
Stranded and Overdyed Floss Cottons	Cement render; flowers; marble, natural stone; painted surfaces; paths; sandstones; sky; slate roof; tiles; window panes
Coton Retors Mat	Bricks (lime washed); cement render; grass; leaves; limestones; paths; plants; terracotta pots; padding for base
Perle Coton	Bricks (wet); plants; flowers; leaves; painted surfaces; water
Dansk Fleur	Brick walls; flowers; leaves; natural stones; paths; tree trunks

STITCHES

Although the designs in this book are worked on a canvas base, since canvas stitches are predominately flat I have incorporated surface stitchery. Texture is important, although it is only one of the many features that enhance the illusion of depth and give life to a piece.

This chapter covers in depth both categories of stitches — canvas and surface — with detailed, graphed instructions for working the individual stitches and for the other techniques that have been employed. I have also included a list of the projects in which I have used a particular stitch or technique.

In the diagrams, the fine lines represent your canvas threads. These must always be counted when working the stitches; **do not count the holes** as some stitches are worked over an odd number of canvas threads.

You do not require a large vocabulary of stitches, only the knowledge of a few basic stitches and the confidence to experiment with them. Changing the direction of the stitch pattern from left to right or from the vertical to the horizontal, adding or subtracting individual stitches within the stitch pattern or working the stitches in a haphazard manner will allow you to form numerous patterns. Repeating or changing a stitch pattern is easier when you understand the principle of the basic pattern.

When changing the direction of a stitch pattern you should remember that a vertical pattern will lengthen an area visually, while a horizontal pattern will widen it.

In this chapter, stitches are listed by name; for example, 'Gobelin'. The basic stitch is explained and some variations on the basic stitch are included under the heading. Where a variation is substantially different to the basic stitch, it has its own title. All instructions are illustrated to help the beginner.

CANVAS STITCHES

In the diagrams in this section the odd numbers represent your threaded needle being brought from the back of the canvas to the front, and even numbers the needle being taken from the front of the canvas to the back.

When a stitch is to be worked over the same number of threads in both directions, there is less chance of an error if you count the canvas intersections rather than the threads.

Wherever possible try to bring the needle from the back of the canvas through an empty hole and return it through a stitched one. The two reasons for not bringing a needle through a previously stitched hole are that you may split the worked thread and that the previous stitch could be pulled forward by the thread, making the surface uneven.

CONTINENTAL

Used in the following projects:
1 Garden Wall
2 Gate in the Wall
3 Hollyhock Cottage
7 Red Window
8 Picket Fence

This stitch can be used with tapestry wool on a 12-count mesh or larger; with a smaller mesh size you must use a lighter weight thread to minimise the distortion.

Although the diagram shows the stitch starting from the right-hand side and working in rows downwards, once you fully understand the stitching, you may start from the left-hand side or work from the bottom up.

If you have any difficulty working this stitch from the diagram, remember that when working from right to left, stitch from the bottom to the top; when working from left to right, stitch from the top to the bottom.

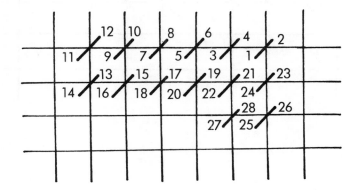

Irregular Continental

Used in the following projects:
1 Garden Wall
8 Picket Fence

With this stitch there is no set pattern, but the angle of the stitch must always be the same no matter what the stitch length. To ensure that the angle is always correct count the canvas thread intersections.

When deciding on the size of the stitch, take into consideration the overall size of the design, the actual area to be worked in the stitch and the mesh size of the canvas, as too large a stitch in a small area will appear out of proportion with the rest of the design. My choice of stitch length is over one, two or three canvas intersections, with a maximum of over four on 14-count canvas. This stitch is excellent for areas of sky or water.

The diagram gives an example only, as you will work to your own pattern. With a careful combination of stitch lengths and working rows across the canvas, not in blocks, the stitch pattern will not be interrupted by too many straight edges.

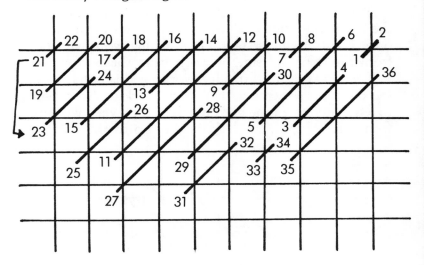

GOBELIN

Interlocking Gobelin

Used in the following projects:
2 Gate in the Wall
3 Hollyhock Cottage
5 Wishing Well
6 Column
7 Red Window

This stitch has a vertical pattern, with the stitch direction running from bottom left to top right. It is always worked over two horizontal threads and one vertical thread. To start the second and subsequent new rows, count down one horizontal thread. The new stitch is then taken over two threads and will fall between the stitches of the previous row. As this stitch has a weak pattern, it is very useful for areas that are flat, such as window panes, lawns and paths. The size of stitch to use will depend on whether the stitch is to be worked in the foreground or the distance.

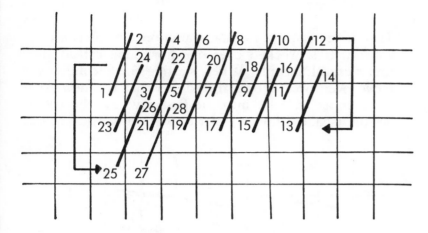

Horizontal Interlocking Gobelin

Used in project:
6 Column

This is basically the same as interlocking gobelin except that the stitch is horizontal rather than vertical and you work the stitches over one horizontal and two vertical rows.

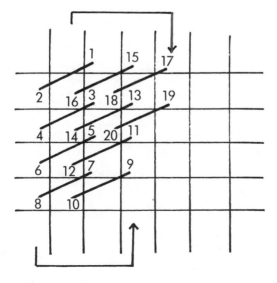

Giant Horizontal Interlocking Gobelin

Used in the following projects:
1 Garden Wall
4 Garden Path
6 Column
8 Picket Fence

This is a giant horizontal variation of interlocking gobelin. It is worked over one horizontal thread and four vertical threads. When starting the second row, move over two vertical threads so that the new row of stitching will slot into the first row. As the stitch lies on its side, I find it easier to work in vertical rows.

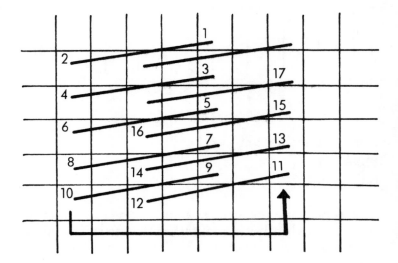

Giant Vertical Interlocking Gobelin

Used in project:
7 Red Window

This stitch is basically interlocking gobelin, but it is worked over four threads, with the stitch direction running from bottom right to top left.

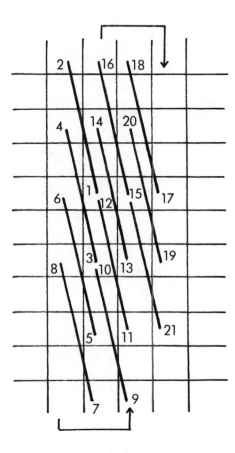

Slanted Gobelin

Used in the following projects:
3 Hollyhock Cottage
5 Wishing Well
7 Red Window

Basic slanted gobelin stitch is worked over two horizontal and two vertical threads (remember it is easier to count the intersections) and forms a series of rows. Ideal for the effect of timber panels, windows and weatherboards.

Quite often an area calls for a slanted stitch on another angle. To achieve the desired angle, adjust the number of canvas threads the stitch is worked over; for example, the roof of the wishing well (project 5) and the window sill of the red window (project 7).

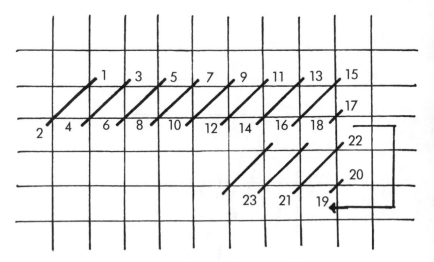

A

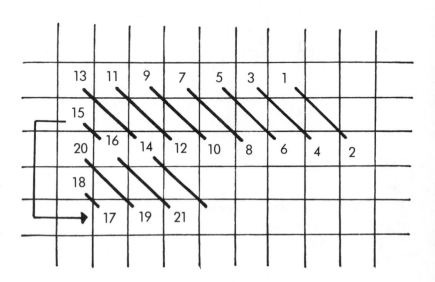

B

Vertical Slanted Gobelin

Used in the following projects:
2 Gate in the Wall
8 Picket Fence

This is a slanted gobelin stitch worked in vertical rows, which makes it very effective for giving the illusion of wood panels, such as the door in project 2 and the single panels of the fence in project 8. As with other stitch patterns, the direction of the stitch may be changed.

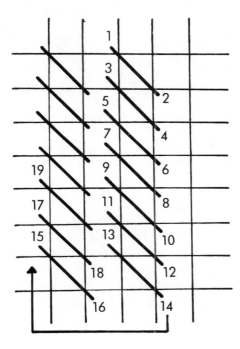

CASHMERE

Brick Wall Cashmere

Used in the following projects:
3 Hollyhock Cottage
5 Wishing Well

The pattern of cashmere stitch gives a rectangular shape that is perfect for the illusion of bricks. The basic cashmere pattern has one pattern shape directly on top of another, but for this variation an extra stitch is added, which allows the bricks to be staggered as in a wall. For a straight edge the end sections of the alternate rows will have to be filled with compensating stitches. If you are unsure of how to compensate, stitch the bulk of the area keeping the pattern of staggered rows flowing, and fill the gaps at the end.

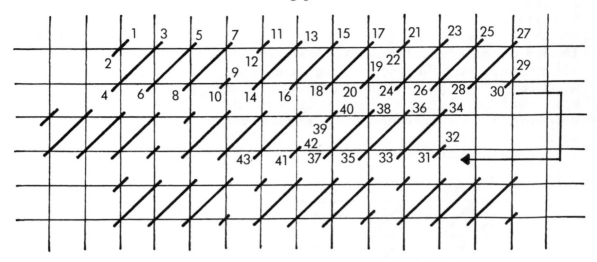

Brick Wall with Mortar

Used in project:
1 Garden Wall

With this variation the rectangle is lengthened with an extra stitch and staggered as before, but it is surrounded by single continental stitches to represent the mortar. Fill the entire area, leaving a single bare canvas thread around each brick; this will then be stitched with continental.

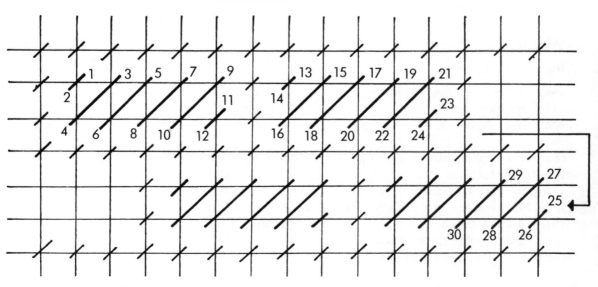

Random Cashmere

Used in the following projects:
2 Gate in the Wall
5 Wishing Well
6 Column
7 Red Window
8 Picket Fence

This pattern represents a sandstone wall and, although I have placed it in the cashmere category, it is actually a combination of different stitches: cashmere, mosaic, and scotch. There is no set pattern to follow, the area is worked with the stitches at random, but take care that the stone edges do not align to form too long a straight line. A true stone wall has to have the stones interlocking otherwise it will collapse.

In areas that call for a stone or brick effect, but cashmere stitch pattern will not fit (for example, projects 5 and 6), adjust the basic stitch by adding length or depth until it fits the area.

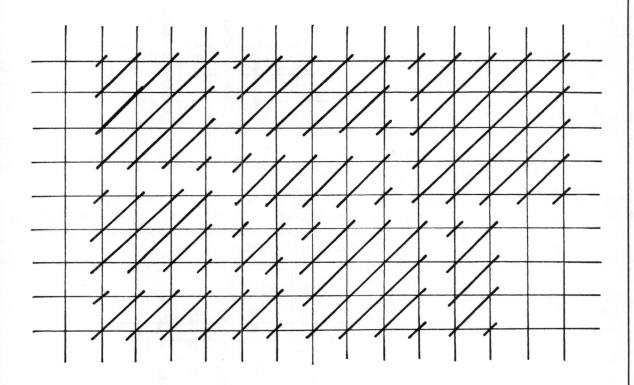

Padded Cashmere

Cashmere is usually a flat stitch, but sometimes it needs to be raised to offset the surrounding stitches. There are various ways to pad stitching, with extra layers of stitching being the simplest. Any number of layers may be stitched under the final surface; it all depends on how far you wish the completed stitch to be raised. The front stones of the wishing well in project 5 have two layers of padding, while the stones of the wall in project 6 have a single layer of padding.

Work the padding as follows.

1. Choose a thread — the thickness will depend on how heavy you wish the padding to be — in a similar colour to the final thread.

2. Work straight stitches from edge to edge of the pattern area. The direction of the padding stitches will depend on the direction of the final stitches.

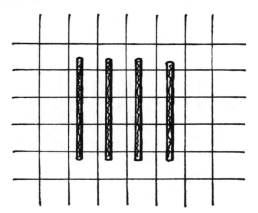

3. If you require a second layer of padding, stitch another layer of straight stitches in the opposite direction to the first.

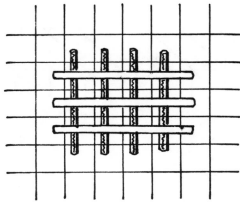

4. Stitch the final layer; with cashmere stitch this will be a diagonal stitch. If you are using stranded cotton, make sure you use enough strands and that they are stripped to give good coverage.

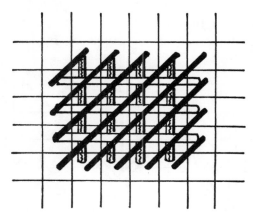

The diagram shows two layers of padding; if only one layer is required, then follow the first step, omit the second and work the top layer of stitches in the same way. The principle is the same for any size of stitch.

CROSS

Used in the following projects:
1 Garden Wall
4 Garden Path

There are many variations of cross stitch and the only requirement is that the top stitch always crosses in the same direction. Below are four variations; the stitches can be combined and overlapped when stitching to make a textured surface.

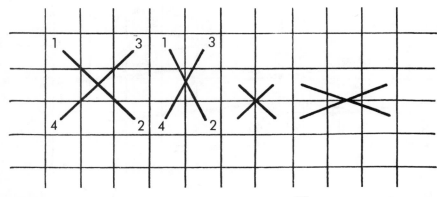

Ermine

Used in project:
1 Garden Wall

With this stitch a basic cross stitch is worked over a vertical straight stitch. You can vary this stitch by moving the cross up or down or by lengthening the vertical stitch.

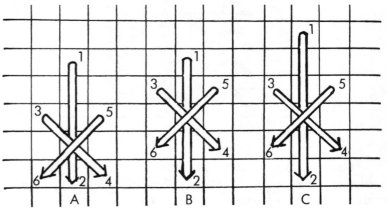

Double Stitch Variation

Used in project:
5 Wishing Well

This stitch is very useful for ground areas where a slightly bumpy texture is required. The pattern forms diagonal rows made by alternating a row of single cross stitches with a row of elongated cross stitches. The rule of the top cross always going in the same direction applies to this variation. I find it easier to work from the bottom up, working one part of the stitch as I go up, then completing the cross as I return.

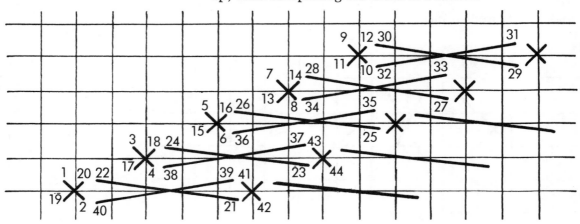

MILANESE

Used in project:
5 Wishing Well

Milanese stitch is a series of triangles that are worked in diagonal rows. An individual triangle pattern consists of four stitches worked diagonally over one, two, three and four intersections. A line of the triangles forms a diagonal row, and the subsequent row has the point of the triangle facing in the opposite direction, which allows the triangles to slot together.

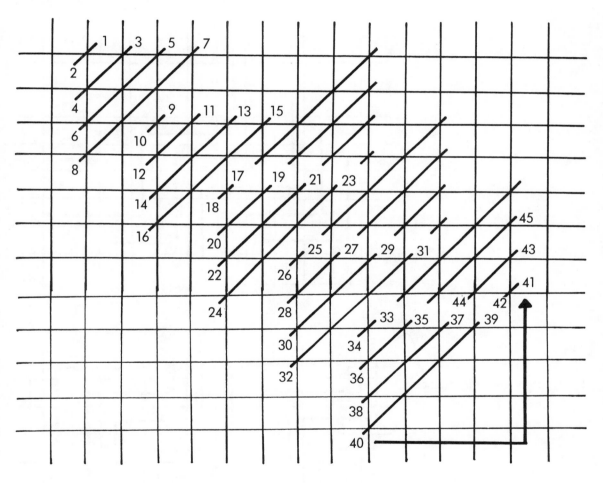

TWILL

Used in project:
6 Column

The overall pattern of this stitch forms a diagonal line. The stitches are worked over three canvas threads, with each new stitch moving up one thread, and the rows alternating between vertical and horizontal stitches.

The dotted lines in the diagram below show the compensating stitches worked to fit the stitch into an area with straight edges, such as the border of a project.

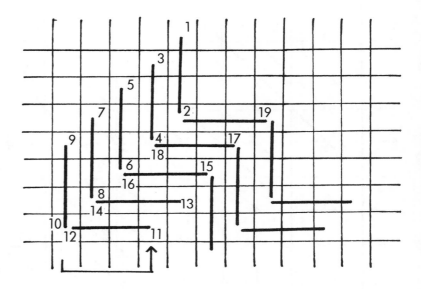

A

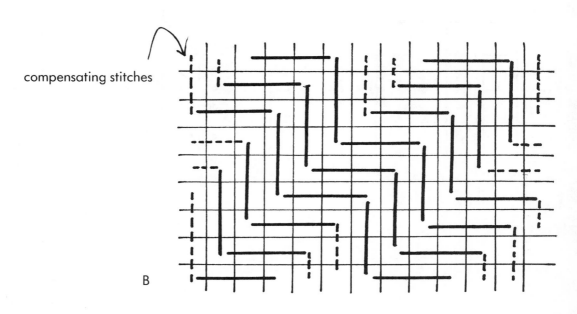

compensating stitches

B

DIAMOND RAY

Random Diamond Ray

Used in project:
2 Gate in the Wall

This pattern is classified as a leaf stitch. It is an arrangement of five straight stitches that share the same base. Where a number of stitches share the same hole, work the stitches by bringing the thread through to the front on the outer edge of the stitch, and work the stitches from alternate sides. This will ensure that the stitches lie flat and no splitting of the threads occurs. In the diagram below the upright stitch is worked first, then the stitch to the left, followed by the one on the right, the lower stitch on the left, and finally the lower stitch on the right. Each time you will be going down through the same hole. The best effect is achieved by working this stitch at random, allowing some of the stitches to overlap.

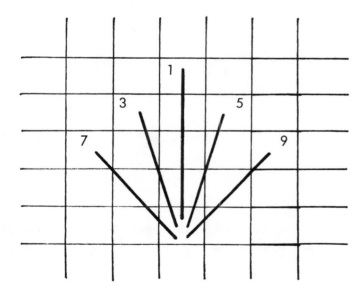

Diamond Ray Variation

Used in the following projects:
2 Gate in the Wall
3 Hollyhock Cottage

With this stitch the base pattern is a diamond ray consisting of three stitches that is turned to face downwards. It is very effective for three pointed leaves such as ivy. To give a natural effect, work the stitching at random in the three directions, allowing the stitches to build up and overlap each other.

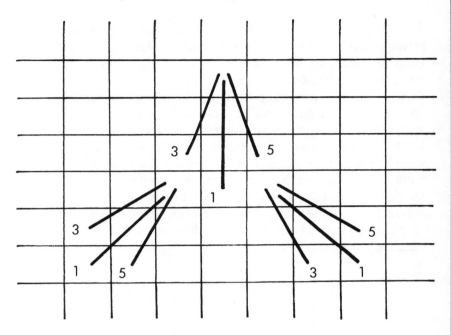

STRAIGHT STITCH

This stitch can be worked both as a canvas stitch and as a surface stitch. I have used it in both ways in the projects.

Horizontal Straight

Used in project:
4 Garden Path

This is a useful stitch for surfaces that are flat, such as grass, water, sky, etc. The diagram below is only a sample of how you could stitch an area. As with irregular continental stitch, do not have too many of the stitches ending in a line, but stagger them.

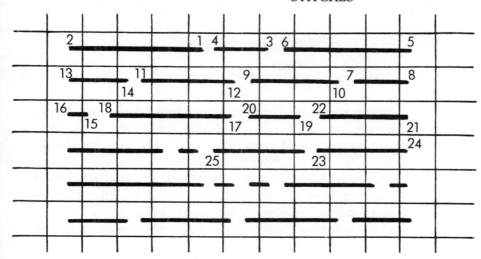

Straight (Plants)

Used in the following projects:
2 Gate in the Wall
4 Garden Path
5 Wishing Well
8 Picket Fence

This is very similar to diamond ray stitch, but with several stitches sharing the same hole at the base. Any number of stitches of differing lengths can be worked. As this stitch is usually worked over other stitching to represent clumps of foliage, it is easier to work from the base to the outside (as the arrows indicate) rather than the other way. This stitch is an exception to the rule where several stitches are worked into the same hole. In this instance the thread is brought from the back through the same hole for all stitches.

To represent flowers, work other stitches at the top of some of the individual straight stitches.

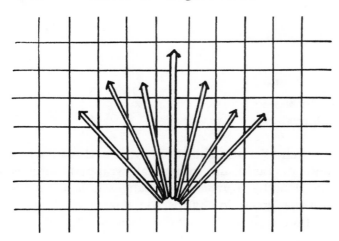

Straight (Thatch)

Used in project:
3 Hollyhock Cottage

When roofs are thatched, you can see the layers of straw at the edges. To achieve this effect with embroidery, use an overdyed wool and work one row of straight stitches over four canvas threads. Move up one canvas thread and, splitting the stitches of the first row, stitch another row of straight stitches over four threads. Repeat this process twice, then move up two canvas threads for each subsequent row until the area is filled.

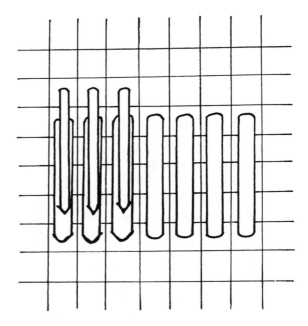

Wrapped Straight

Used in project:
6 Column

This stitch is a straight stitch with a thread wrapped around it. Build up individual wrapped stitches of varying lengths from a single canvas hole to duplicate a plant that grows in clumps, like flax.

To stitch a clump follow the steps on page 45:

1. Work a single straight stitch.
2. Bring the needle from the back of the canvas at the base of the stitch and wrap the thread around the stitch until it is completely covered. Take the thread to the back of the canvas at the top of the straight stitch.
3. Repeat the process until you have the entire plant.

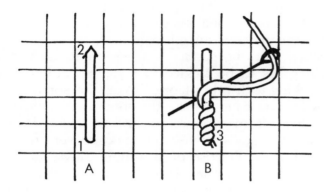

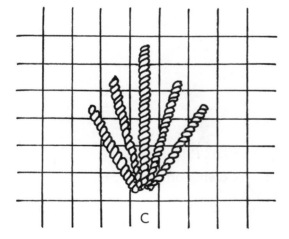

SURFACE STITCHES

Traditionally, surface stitches were worked to a regimented size and style, often in precise lines of stitching. However, in this book I have taken individual stitches and worked them at random to give textural relief. With my type of stitching, you rarely have to unpick your work, for when a stitch is too large, you overlap it with the next.

In this section the diagrams show the threads lying on top of the canvas and, if you look carefully, you will see how one thread goes under another when being worked. When the stitch is shown with a blunt end it represents a thread being brought from the back of the canvas to the front: when there is an arrow, it represents a thread taken through that canvas hole to the back of the work. In some instances it is necessary to have the needle brought to the front of the work, or at least positioned for the next stage of the stitch, before the previous stitch is tightened.

When working surface stitches on to canvas, the stitching has to be tackled in a slightly different way to working with other fabric. To anchor some stitches in place, you have to take the stitch over a thread of the canvas. In many cases you will be unable to count the canvas threads, as you are working over previously stitched areas. Practise on a sample canvas until you are confident with the stitch, then when you work on the proper canvas you will be able to gauge the stitch by eye.

RANDOM FLY STITCH

Used in the following projects:
1 Garden Wall
2 Gate in the Wall
4 Garden Path
5 Wishing Well
6 Column
8 Picket Fence

Fly stitch looks like the letter 'Y'; the version I use has a shorter tail than is usual, as it is only required to hold the initial stitch in place. This stitch is used where you want a textured surface with only basic shading. When used among flat stitches, it will come forward; while among textured stitches, it will recede.

The diagram on page 47 shows the procedure for an individual fly stitch.

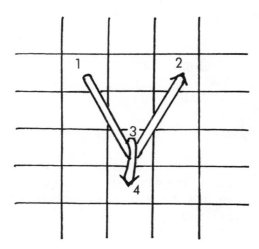

1. Bring the needle from the back of the canvas at 1.

2. Counting over two canvas threads, take the needle back through the canvas hole at 2; do not tighten the thread, but form it into a loop.

3. Bring the needle back to the front through canvas hole 3, making sure the needle is above the loop, then tighten the loop to form a V.

4. Anchor the V stitch by taking the needle over a canvas thread and through the canvas at 4.

To work an area, fill it with individual stitches worked haphazardly and overlapping each other as shown below.

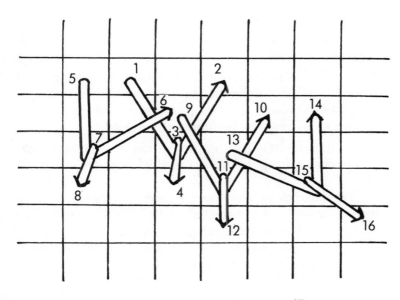

CHAIN

Detached Chain

Used in the following projects:
1 Garden Wall
2 Gate in the Wall
4 Garden Path
8 Picket Fence

This stitch resembles a closed horseshoe or an oval ring. Unlike fly stitch, it forms a distinct stitch that is suitable for stitching in the foreground. The depth of texture of this stitch depends on the type of thread used.

The diagram below shows you how to form an individual stitch.

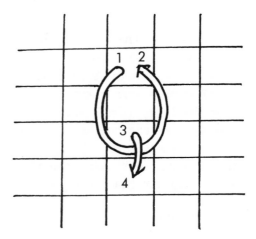

1. Bring the needle from the back of the canvas at 1.
2. Forming a loop with your thread, take the needle to the back of the canvas through the same hole (2).
3. Count down two canvas threads and bring your needle to the front of the canvas, with the thread passing through the loop formed and the needle above the loop. Now tighten the thread.
4. Anchor the loop by counting down one canvas thread and then taking the needle to the back at 4.

The diagram at the top of page 49 shows how to form stitches that are started to the left and right. The basic procedure is the same as above.

You can also overlap the stitches. As with fly stitch, to build up an area work the base stitches at random.

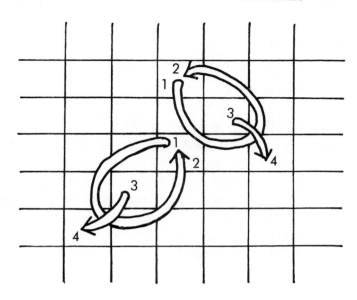

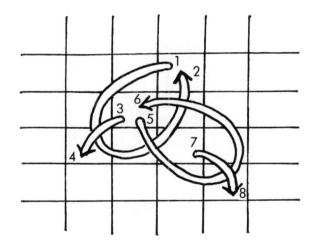

Detached Twisted Chain

Used in the following projects:
1 Garden Wall
4 Garden Path
5 Wishing Well
6 Column
8 Picket Fence

With a simple change in stitching procedure a chain
stitch becomes raised, thus forming a twisted chain,

which is predominantly used in the foreground of any work.

The diagram below shows how you form an individual stitch.

1. Bring your needle from the back of the canvas at 1.

2. Form a loop and take your needle over the looped thread. Pass to the back of the canvas at 2.

3. Bring your needle from the back of the canvas, at 3, bringing the thread through the loop formed. Tighten the loop.

4. To anchor the stitch, take the needle over the loop, across a canvas thread and through to the back of the canvas at 4.

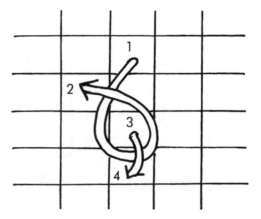

The diagram below shows how to form the stitches that are started to the left and right.

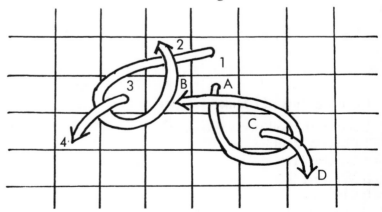

You can also overlap the stitches as with basic detached chain stitch. To fill in an area, combine the stitches at random.

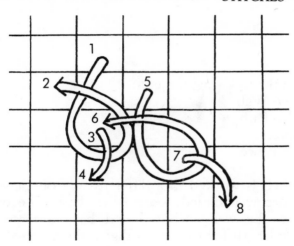

Individual Raised Chain Band

Used in the following projects:
1 Garden Wall
2 Gate in the Wall

Most of this stitch is worked on the surface. It has a single straight stitch that lies on top of the canvas, with a raised chain stitch being worked over the straight stitch.
Work this stitch as follows.

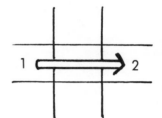

1. Bring the needle from the back of the canvas at 1 and, counting over two threads, take the needle through to the back of the canvas at 2. This forms the base of the stitch.

2. Position your needle in the canvas hole in the centre of the band (3) and above the thread, before tightening the first stitch.

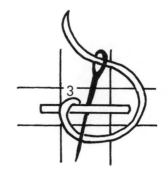

3. Bring the needle through to the front with the thread on the left side and form a loop over the band by taking the thread to the right above the band.

4. Take the needle under the straight stitch just to the right of 3, passing it over the looped thread.

5. Pull the thread firmly, but not so tight that the straight stitch loses its shape. Now take the needle over a canvas thread and through to the back of the canvas at 4 to anchor the stitch.

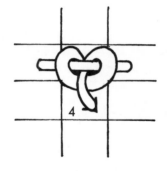

If you carefully position the threads on this stitch, you will form the iris flower.

KNOTS

Bullion

Used in the following projects:
1 Garden Wall
4 Garden Path
6 Column
8 Picket Fence

This stitch is worked in a different way on canvas to embroidering it directly on a fabric base. The thread needs to be well anchored and have a reasonable working length for the twists that make up the stitch.
On canvas, form the stitch as follows.

1. Bring the needle from the back of the canvas at 1 and, leaving a loop, take the needle through to the back at 2. Do not pull the thread tight.

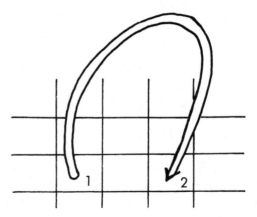

2. Bring part of the needle through to the front at the starting point 1 and wrap the loop of the thread around the needle a number of times.

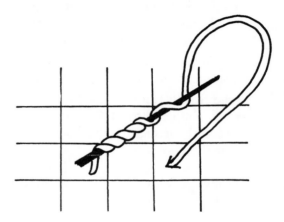

3. Holding the twisted thread in position, pull the needle through. Tighten the twists along the thread until all the slack has been taken up.

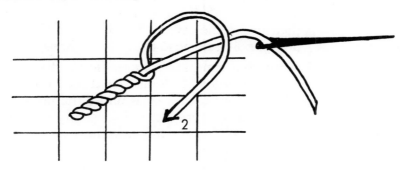

4. When the stitch is firm, take the needle to the back of the canvas through the same hole (2).

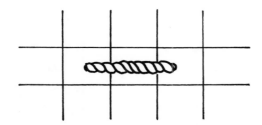

Colonial Knot

Used in the following projects:
1 Garden Wall
2 Gate in the Wall
4 Garden Path
5 Wishing Well
6 Column
8 Picket Fence

This forms a fairly thick knot, so it is useful for flowers, plants and sheep. Stitch it at random otherwise you will find that rows will appear when you are filling in an area.

Work this stitch as described on the following page.

1. Bring the needle from the back of the canvas to the front at 1.

2. Holding the thread towards you with the needle tip pointing away from you, take the needle tip over, then under the thread. Keep hold of the needle and do not pull it through the twisted thread at this point.

3. With your right index finger (left index finger if you are left-handed) holding the thread on the needle, take the thread over then under the needle tip. This will form a figure eight. Pull gently on the thread, then place the needle into the canvas one canvas thread away at 2.

4. As you pull the needle through, keep a firm pressure on the thread, until it forms a knot.

A

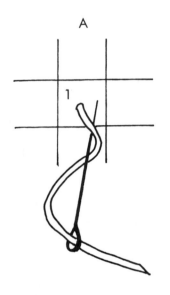

B

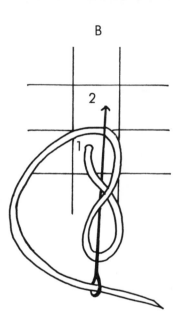

C

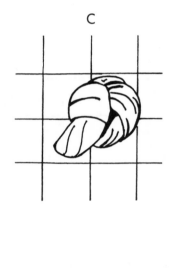

French Knot

Used in the following projects:
3 Hollyhock Cottage
5 Wishing Well
6 Column

This is a small knot used for the centre of flowers, individual small flowers and plants, or in combination

with colonial knots to vary a textured surface.
Work this stitch as follows.

1. Bring the needle from the back of the canvas to the front at 1.
2. Hold the thread at an angle of 90 degrees to the canvas.
3. Hold the needle horizontally and wrap the thread around the needle tip once.
4. Keeping a firm pressure on the thread, position the needle into the canvas at 2, moving over one canvas thread from 1.
5. Hold the thread firmly until the needle is at the back and the knot is formed.

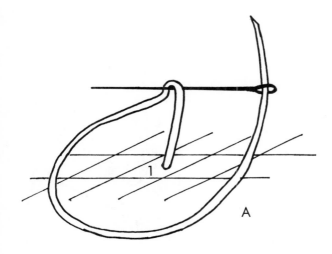

A

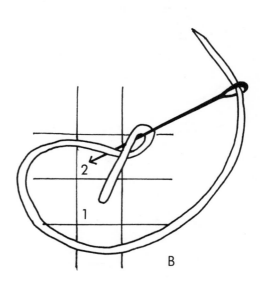

B

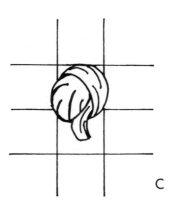

C

Pistil

Used in the following projects:
1 Garden Wall
6 Column
8 Picket Fence

This stitch is a French knot with a tail. The tail can be any length to suit the design. The stitch is worked in the same way as a French knot, but you take the needle to the back two or more canvas threads away from the starting point in any direction. The knot will rest at the end of the tail at the point where the thread goes back through the canvas (2).

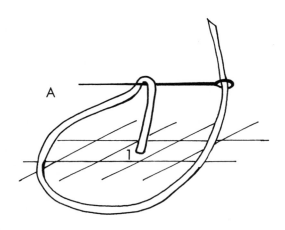

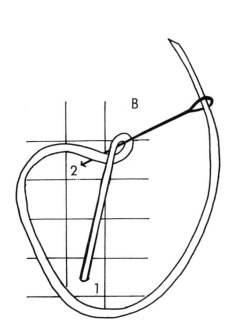

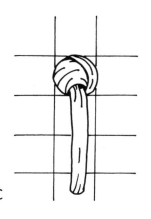

Coral Knot

Used in project:
4 Garden Path

This stitch is made up of a series of knots worked in a line. In project 4 coral stitch is used to represent weeds growing between stones of a garden path, but it could also be used for trailing vines. This stitch can be worked in any direction.
  Work this stitch as follows.

1. Bring the needle through from the back at 1. With the thread forming a loop to the left, take the needle over the top of the loop and insert it back into the canvas at 2.
2. Bring the needle back through the canvas and the loop at 3, one canvas thread down from 2.
3. Lay the thread on the canvas to the left of the previous stitch and hold it in place with your fingers.
4. Take the needle over the thread and insert it back through the canvas at 4 to form a second loop.
5. Bring the needle up through the canvas and the loop at 5, one canvas thread down from 4 and pull the thread firmly to complete the knot.
6. Repeat steps 3, 4 and 5 until the line is completed.

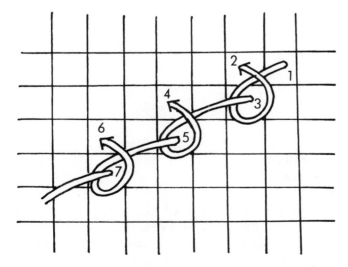

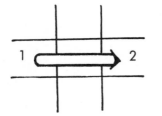

Palestrina

Used in the following projects:
1 Garden Wall
8 Picket Fence

This stitch is similar to the individual raised chain band, as it is also worked over a straight stitch or band.
    Work the knot as follows.

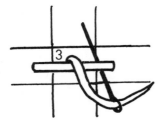

1. Make a straight stitch over two canvas threads to form the base of the knot.
2. Bring the needle from the back through the central hole (3) with the thread above the base stitch. Have the thread hanging down over the straight stitch and take the needle under the band to the right of the thread.

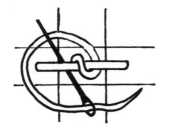

3. Form a loop of thread that lies above the band and to the left of the twist you have already made and bring the needle under the left side of the straight stitch and over the looped thread.
4. Pull the thread so that the knot is firm and anchor it by taking the needle to the back of the canvas at 4, one canvas thread above.

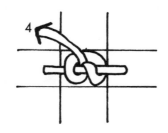

FERN

Used in project:
2 Gate in the Wall

This stitch is made up of three individual straight stitches. The first stitch is worked diagonally over two canvas intersections and the other two stitches are worked into the same canvas hole as the centre stitch.
    The diagram at the top of page 59 shows a diagonal line of fern stitch, but it may be worked in any direction or as a wavy line. The stitches may be any length.

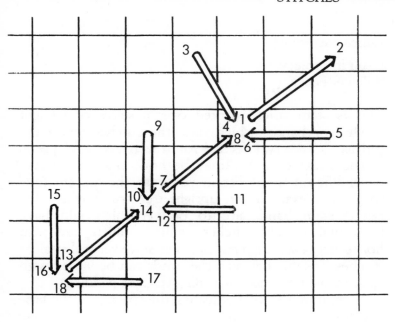

STEM

Basic Stem

Used in project:
1 Garden Wall

Stem stitch is usually used for outlines or, as its name implies, the stems of plants or small branches. Depending on the thickness and type of the thread used and how close together the stitches are worked it can also represent rope.

The stitch is very pliable, as it is a series of small stitches of equal length. When working stem stitch, be careful to keep the thread below the needle so that the stitches are always on the same side.

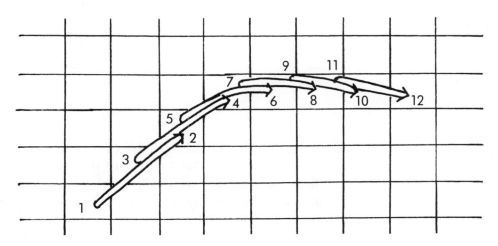

Raised Stem Band

Used in project:
8 Picket Fence

This is stem stitch worked over a series of straight stitches or bands, which raise the stitches above the canvas. It is very effective for tree trunks and posts.

The straight stitches may be horizontal or vertical, depending on the direction you wish the top stitching to go. For example, an upright tree trunk where the raised stem bands are to be vertical would have horizontal straight stitches, while a fallen tree with horizontal raised stem bands would have vertical straight stitches. Spacing between the bands can be varied with close straight stitches; this will give extra padding.

Note, however, that adjusting the spacing of the base stitches will vary the size of the top stitches. Once you feel confident about the basic stitching, experiment with various combinations of colours and threads.

Work the stitches as follows.

1. Fill the area with parallel straight stitches.

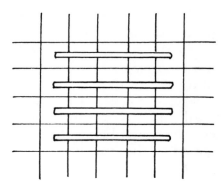

2. Bring the thread through the canvas from the back at the bottom left-hand corner of the area.
3. Take the thread to the right of the point you came up and bring the needle down under the first straight stitch from above.

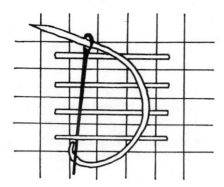

4. Pull the thread taut.

5. Place the thread to the right of the needle again and bring it down under the second straight stitch from above. Pull the thread taut.

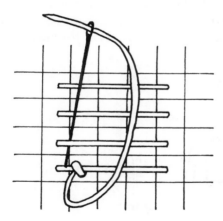

6. Repeat step 5 until you have reached the top of the straight stitches.

7. After the stitch is worked on the uppermost straight stitch, take the needle through to the back and anchor the thread.

8. Start from the bottom again and, working to the right of the first set of stitches, proceed to stitch to the top. Repeat this process until the bands are filled, then work one more row. This ensures that the stitches push against each other, bringing the stitched area forward, which intensifies the feeling of depth.

WRAPPED THREADS

Used in project:
6 Column

This stitch is to get a three-dimensional effect for such things as vines. The base thread you choose will depend on the finished thickness you require and the length of this should be one and a half times the finished length of the stitch. The steps given below are repeated for each vine.

1. Anchor both the base and wrapping threads on the back of the canvas at the bottom of the area.
2. Bring both threads to the front of the canvas.
3. Holding the base thread, twist the wrapping thread firmly around it until it is the required length. The more firmly you wrap the thread, the more natural the effect you will obtain.
4. Take both threads through to the back of the canvas at the top of the area and anchor them. Attach the wrapped thread at selected positions with a couching stitch (small stitch to anchor thread) to hold it in place.

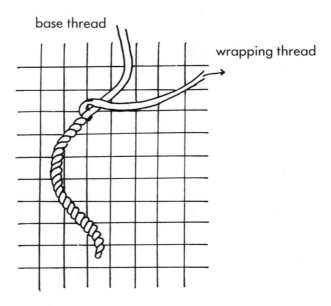

base thread

wrapping thread

BUTTONHOLE

Detached Buttonhole

Used in project:
3 Hollyhock Cottage

This stitch forms a circle or oval. You can work partial detached buttonhole stitches to represent half flowers or buds. The stitches are worked so that the centre of the flower is fixed to the canvas and the outer stitches are free to protrude or bow.
   Work the stitch as follows.

1. Work two parallel straight stitches in the same canvas channel.

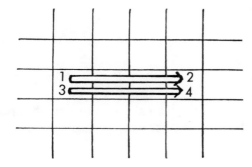

2. Bring your needle through from the back of the canvas at 5, above the top straight stitch. Form a loop by laying your thread to the right of 5 above the straight stitches.

3. With the needle pointing upwards, take the needle under the top straight stitch, passing it over the loop of thread. Tighten the thread gently.

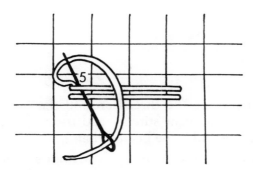

4. Form another loop of thread to the right of the first stitch, above the straight stitch. Take the needle under the stitch and over the loop in the same way as in steps 2 and 3.

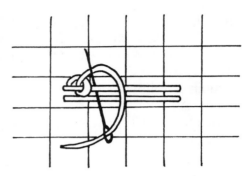

5. Continue working loops over the straight stitch until you reach the end of the top straight stitch.

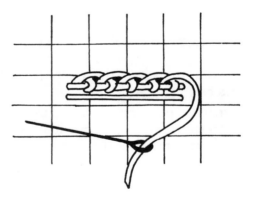

6. To turn, bring the thread around the outside of the end of the straight stitches and form a loop that lies to the left under the bottom band.

7. With the needle pointing downwards, take it under the bottom straight stitch and over the loop.

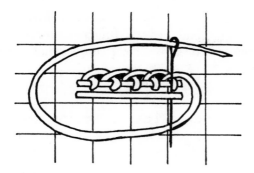

8. Repeat step 7 until the bottom straight stitch is completely covered. Then take the needle through to the back at 6 immediately next to your starting point.

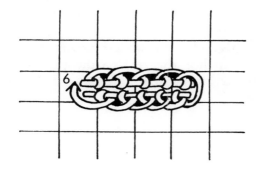

Buttonhole Rings

Used in project:
5 Wishing Well

You can make individual buttonhole rings, which can be used for a multitude of effects. Certain threads and the size of the base circle may cause the rings to twist on themselves and this feature can be used when attached to the canvas with a few stitches to form a

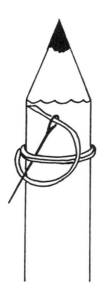

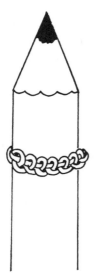

heavily textured area that is very effective in the foreground of a scene. Pencils, fingers or wooden dowels are just a few of the cylindrical shapes that are suitable to use as a base.

Work the rings as follows.

1. Choose a cylindrical base of the diameter you want the ring to be and, ensuring you have a reasonable length of thread, wrap the thread around it twice.

2. Holding the thread firmly around the base, allow it to hang down and form a loop below the wrapped thread. Bring the needle down under the wrapped threads, over the loop and pull the needle through.

3. Form another loop of thread below the wrapped threads and bring the needle down under the wrapped thread and over the loop again. Pull the needle through and repeat this process until the wrapped base is completely covered.

4. To finish, take the needle through the first loop worked to anchor the stitches, then remove the ring from the base.

5. The length of the thread left attached to the ring is used to anchor the ring to the canvas. The ring can be twisted to form any shape — it need not only be a ring.

Buttonhole on a Knot

Used in the following projects:
6 Column
7 Red Window

This is a very useful stitch to add dimension to a canvas, but it can be overpowering and so its use must be carefully considered in relation to other stitches. It is not worked directly on the canvas but is formed completely separately like crochet (which is an alternative, if you prefer it, although adjustments may be necessary). Altering the number and position of stitches worked will change the shape (for variations see buttonhole leaves and flowers on page 69). As the name implies, this stitch is worked on a base knot, which when formed must be firm enough to work three stitches into it with ease.

The following instructions are for the leaves and flowers in project 7.

1. Start with a reasonable length of thread (approximately 25 cm [10 in] long). Make a knot near the end of the thread but leave enough thread to hold onto while stitching and to take to the back of the work when the shape is completed.

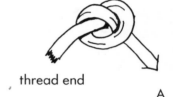

thread end

A

2. To make the first row, bring the length of thread from the right anti-clockwise around the knot to the bottom, then take the needle through the centre of the knot, passing the needle above the thread. Pull the thread through to form a buttonhole stitch. Diagram C shows the needle positioned for the next buttonhole stitch.

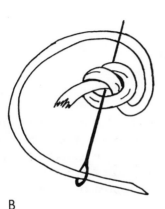

B

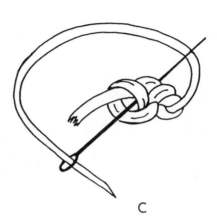

C

3. Make three buttonhole stitches into the knot following step 2.

4. For the second row, work buttonhole stitches into the first row of stitches, making two stitches into the first and last stitches of the previous row. You will now have five buttonhole stitches in this row.

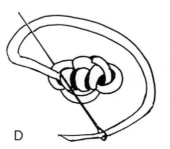

D

start of second row

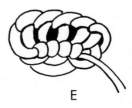

E

end of second row

5. Work the third row in the same way as the previous rows, adding an extra stitch in the first and last stitches of the previous row, making a total of seven stitches in all.

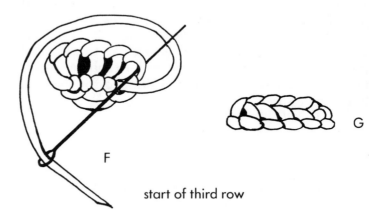

F

G

start of third row

6. The finished shape forms a small cup. Weave the working thread through to the knot, then use this thread to anchor the shape to the canvas in the required position. In project 7 they are positioned with the curve downwards to represent flowers and leaves.

Buttonhole Flowers

Used in project:
6 Column

The same procedure is followed for this stitch as for the buttonhole on a knot, but the number and position of stitches differs.

1. Start with a knot and stitch into the centre of the knot in the same way as described for the buttonhole on a knot, working eight stitches in a circle.
2. Take the working thread through the top of the first stitch and weave it back to the centre of the circle. Use the thread to anchor the flower in place.

The flower shape may be altered by changing the number and position of the buttonhole stitches.

Buttonhole Leaves

Used in project:
6 Column

This is yet another variation on the buttonhole on a knot. It is worked as follows.

1. Starting with a knot, work a circle of eight stitches around the knot as for the buttonhole flower.
2. Make buttonhole stitches into the first five stitches of the previous row.
3. For the third row, turn and work three stitches into the second row, missing the second and fourth stitches.
4. Turn and work one stitch into the middle stitch of the third row.
5. Weave the working thread through to the knot, and once you have sewn the flower into position on the leaf so that the tip of the point shows, then use the working thread to anchor the bottom edge of the leaf to the canvas. The shape of the leaf should be round at the bottom edge and pointed at the top.

OTHER TECHNIQUES

Combining other techniques with canvas and surface stitches will help to give your work visual impact. However, it is only possible to use a fairly free interpretation of the true form of the techniques on canvas.

APPLIQUÉ

Appliqué is adding one or more pieces of fabric to the surface of a foundation fabric to form a design. Stitching can only be raised a little way above the foundation fabric, but, with this technique, different levels of stitching as well as other materials can be introduced to your work.

CROCHET AND KNITTING

When crochet or knitting are mentioned, garments spring to mind, but small shapes are easily worked using either technique and can be incorporated into your work to obtain different effects.

RAISED WORK

Also known as stumpwork, this is a three-dimensional effect achieved by padding, using moulds, wadding or concealed stitches.

In project 6, the column is the focal point of the design and needs to be bold. Initially when considering the design, I thought of working raised stem band, but I decided that this would not be prominent enough. I wanted a stone or marble effect, which would require a stitch that was smooth but would stand out from the background without dominating the area. The only solution was to stitch a separate piece of canvas and appliqué it to the main canvas.

PROJECTS

This chapter contains eight projects or scenes to be worked on canvas. For each scene I have given a design outline that you can trace on your canvas, together with a list of the stitches, threads and colours that I used. Where no specified number of strands has been listed, a single strand is to be used. In a number of projects, multiple colour numbers are given for a thread. These should be worked separately and at random over the marked area unless it is specified that they be threaded in the same needle. For ease of working, I have also listed the areas in their stitching order.

The illustrated scenes are only examples of what can be done and they have been designed so that you can change the thread colours or sections of stitching as you wish. For example, in Project 1, Garden Wall, you may wish to change the brick wall with mortar to a sandstone wall or a plain brick wall without mortar. One point to remember is that if you are changing a colour in one area, always check that the new shade is compatible with the other colours and, if necessary, change them as well. Take care that the colours you choose are of different values and that you get a variety, from light to dark, subtle to strong.

When you trace the design on your canvas, it is not necessary to transfer the letters. These are given to indicate the order in which you stitch the scene and to link the areas with the working instructions.

A few of the threads that I recommend may be unavailable and, as it is always difficult to duplicate a colour and thread, I have listed below some possible alternatives.

● Dansk Fleur may be substituted with DMC Danish Flower

Dansk Fleur	DMC Danish Flower
15	2405
29	2497
32	2241
33	2775
100	2986
113	2758
232	2728
237	2469
238	2937/2986

● Knitting Wool: Zig may be substituted by DMC stranded cotton and coton retors mat twisted together.

Zig	Stranded cotton with Coton retors mat
Green/Brown	936/838 with 2898 Green/2840 Brown
Green/Gold	832/732 with 2832 Green

When experimenting with the colour combinations, remember that the coton retors mat is the base colour and only one strand is used. Depending on the dominant colour you wish to achieve, add more or less of the stranded cotton colours. Adjust the colour with single strands of stranded cotton; for example, if green is to be the dominant colour, use 2898 with three strands of 936 and two strands of 838.

1 GARDEN WALL

AREA	STITCH	THREAD/ COLOUR/ NUMBER OF STRANDS
A Sky	Irregular continental	Stranded cotton 828 8 strands
B Wall Bricks	Brick wall with mortar cashmere	Dansk Fleur HF 32/33/232 5 strands
Mortar	Continental	Dansk Fleur HF 15 3 strands
C Path	Giant horizontal interlocking gobelin	Coton retors mat 2233
D Tree	Random fly	Tapestry wool 7379 Zig knitting wool green/brown
E Creeper (middle) Leaves	Ermine	Dansk Fleur HF 237/238 3 strands
Flowers	Cross	Dansk Fleur HF 232 3 strands
F Creeper (left) Leaves	Detached chain	Medici wool 8414 4 strands

AREA	STITCH	THREAD/ COLOUR/ NUMBER OF STRANDS
Flowers	Detached chain	Medici wool 8896/8895/8333 4 strands
G		
Leaves	Detached twisted chain	Perle coton No. 5 895 2 strands
Flowers	Individual raised chain band	Stranded cotton 600 6 strands
H		
Leaves	Detached twisted chain	Tapestry wool 7408
I		
Leaves	Random fly	Perle coton No. 3 936 1 strand Stranded cotton 988/3346 2 strands
Flowers	Palestrina knit	Overdyed cotton 144 6 strands
J		
Leaves	Detached twisted chain	Perle coton No. 5 987 1 strand
Flowers	Bullion knot (vary the number of twists)	Stranded cotton 553
K and L		
Leaves	Colonial knot	Coton retors mat 2907/2906
Long Stemmed Flowers (behind the wall — optional)		
Stems	Stem	Stranded cotton 502/504 2 strands
Flowers	Pistil	Stranded cotton 3726/3727 2 strands

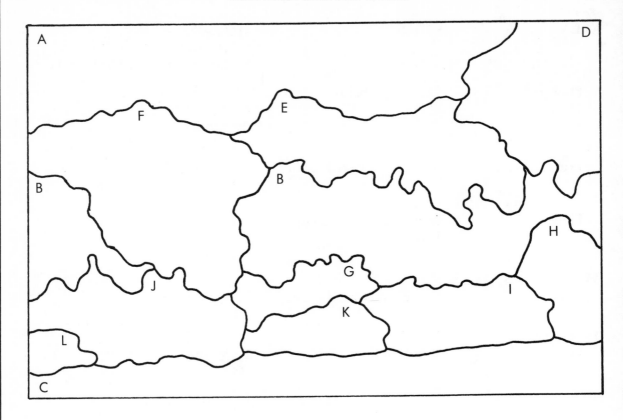

INSTRUCTIONS

Area A (sky)

Strip and use eight strands of the thread, keeping the strands flat to ensure maximum coverage. Take the stitches slightly over the outlines into the plant areas.

Area B (wall)

The bricks have been stitched with five strands and the mortar with three. This helps to create the illusion of the bricks protruding. Take the stitches slightly over the outlines into the plant areas.

Area C (path)

As the path is going from bottom left to top right, make sure your stitch pattern is also flowing in that direction.

Area D (tree)

With the tapestry wool, fill the area, then stitch over the base stitches at random using Zig knitting wool, or

GARDEN WALL

GATE IN THE WALL

HOLLYHOCK COTTAGE

WISHING WELL

COLUMN

RED WINDOW

its substitute, taking some of the stitches back over the sky.

Area E (middle creeper)

Using the dark shade of cotton, scatter your stitching throughout the area with a build up towards the base. Then stitch with the light shade, making sure some of the light threads go over the dark and mingle into the tree (D). The flowers are stitched at random, with more at the top of the area.

Area F (left creeper)

The leaves were worked in one colour but shade changes were introduced into the flowers. Again, scatter the leaves over the stitching of the wall.

Area G (plants)

Fill the area with twisted chain stitch, then scatter the flowers over the area, placing some on the brick wall.

Area H (plants)

Tapestry wool was used in this area to help the feeling of depth. Make sure that the bottom stitches overlap the path slightly.

Area I (plants)

Initially, a base of stitches in perle coton was worked over the area. This was then stitched over with green stranded cotton. Overlap the path with the bottom stitches.

Area J (plants)

Fill the area with detached twisted chain stitch, making sure that the stitches overlap the wall. Work bullion knots, varying the size and number of twists and allowing some stitches to curve slightly. To give the effect of height, the flower stitches should overlap the wall further than the greenery.

Areas K and L (plants)

When stitching the colonial knots, change the tension as well as scattering the areas with the dark and light green.

Long-stemmed flowers (behind the wall)

These are optional. To enhance the feeling of the flowers being in the background, they are worked with two strands of stranded cotton, and to give the impression of both new and mature growth, two shades of green and pink were used.

2 GATE IN THE WALL

AREA	STITCH	THREAD/ COLOUR/ NUMBER OF STRANDS
A Sky	Continental	Stranded cotton 800 6 strands
B Wall 　B1 　B2 　B3	Random cashmere	Overdyed cotton 187 172 171 6 strands each
C Grass	Interlocking gobelin	Coton retors mat 2906/2907
D Gate	Vertical slanted gobelin	Watercolour perle coton blueberry 2 strands
E Tree behind the wall	Random fly	Zig knitting wool green/brown
F Climbing roses 　Leaves	Detached chain	Dansk Fleur 238 3 strands
Flowers	Colonial knot	Stranded cotton 814/815 6 strands

AREA	STITCH	THREAD/ COLOUR/ NUMBER OF STRANDS
G Leaves	Diamond ray variation	Tapestry wool 7702 Coton retors mat 2319/2320
H Iris Leaves	Straight	Perle coton No. 5 890
Flowers	Individual raised chain band	Overdyed cotton MT 110/2 6 strands
I Wavy plant	Fern	Perle coton No. 5 936 2 strands
J Foreground plants	Random diamond ray	Overdyed wool green/brown 2 strands
K Shadow above gate	Continental	Stranded cotton 3371 6 strands
L Shadow under gate	See instructions page 80	

INSTRUCTIONS

When tracing this scene you will notice that some of the outlines are dotted lines. To help give a realistic effect, end the base stitches at the dotted line, then let the surface stitching overlap into the adjacent area, with the base stitching showing through.

The arrows in areas B and D are to indicate in which direction the stitching should flow.

Plants marked H and I need not be traced on your canvas as they are stitched after the wall is completed.

Area A (sky)

Stitch to the outline of area E. If you stitch over the entire sky then work area E over the top; it will protrude and bring the background tree too far forward.

Area B (wall)

This area has been split into three sections: B1, B2 and B3. Each section is stitched in a different shade and direction to give the illusion of an angled surface.

Area C (grass)

To give an impression of the wall's shadow falling on the lawn, two shades of green have been used, with the light shade blending into the dark.

Area D (gate)

Start stitching the gate from the right-hand side and work the stitch pattern over two threads to represent wood panels. Compensate on the last row if necessary.

Area E (tree behind the wall)

Scatter your stitching at the outer edges and, where the canvas is bare, fill in with the sky thread.

Area F (creeper, roses)

First fill the area with green stitches, then, using two shades, scatter the flowers. The flowers should also spill over onto the wall surface.

Area G (creeper, ivy)

Work this area in three stages, in dark, middle and light shades.

Area H (irises)

Vary the length of the straight stitches and work the flowers at the end of a few of them, making sure that the flowers are not all on the same level.

Area I (wavy plant)

Try to curve the fern stitch as you work over the stitched wall to give a realistic effect.

Area J (foreground plants)

To give the impression of rows of plants, work the area in layers from the back to the front. Stitch one row, then drop half the stitch pattern for the next one, to allow the new row to overlap the previous one. For example, if the stitch pattern is over four horizontal threads, the second row will commence two rows down so that the top two rows of the new stitches will overlap into the bottom of the previous row.

Area K (shadow above the gate)

Work this area with a plain stitch and in a dark colour to help give the appearance of a partially open gate.

Area L (shadow under the gate)

This area may be stitched as a continuation of the grass using a darker shade of green or, perhaps, as the start of a path on the other side of the gate. In the latter case, stitch it in the same way as area K, the shadow above the gate.

3 HOLLYHOCK COTTAGE

AREA	STITCH	THREAD/ COLOUR/ NUMBER OF STRANDS
A Windows		
Frame	Continental and slanted gobelin	Perle coton No. 3 white
Panes	Straight	Stranded cotton 318 6 strands
Large pane	Interlocking gobelin	Stranded cotton 413 6 strands
Stone surround	Slanted gobelin	Coton retors mat 2841/2842
B Bricks	Brick wall cashmere	Coton retors mat ecru/2839/2647 2648/2841
C Roof	Straight (thatch)	Overdyed wool shades of brown 2 strands
D Hollyhocks		
Leaves	Diamond ray variation	Perle coton No. 5 320/367/379

AREA	STITCH	THREAD/ COLOUR/ NUMBER OF STRANDS
Flowers	Detached buttonhole	Stranded cotton 3607/3608 6 strands
	French knot	Stranded cotton white 2 strands

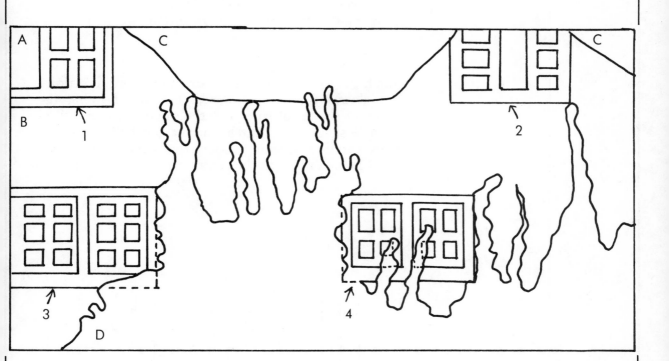

INSTRUCTIONS

With this design there is a separate chart to follow for each window, so only mark the outside line of the windows on your canvas.

Area A *(windows)*

See diagrams 1, 2, 3 and 4 on the following pages. Follow the stitch directions on the individual window graphs.

Area B *(bricks)*

This is an area that could be changed to a different style of wall if you prefer it.

Area C *(thatch)*

For a natural effect use either overdyed wool or two or more shades of thread at the same time. To achieve the effect of thicker thatch at the bottom edge, start at the base of the area and work upwards.

Area D *(hollyhocks)*

Stitch the leaves so that they are in different directions, but always facing downwards. For the flowers, use different shades of thread at the same time, as well as a single shade. Also stitch quarter and half flowers to represent buds opening. Using two strands of cotton, work French knots in the centre of the flowers.

1

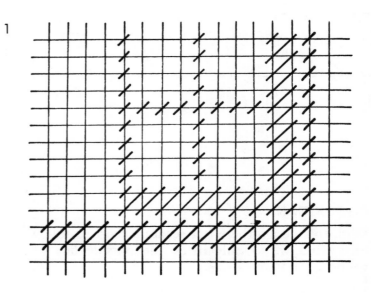

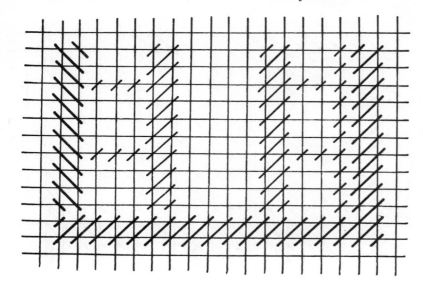

2

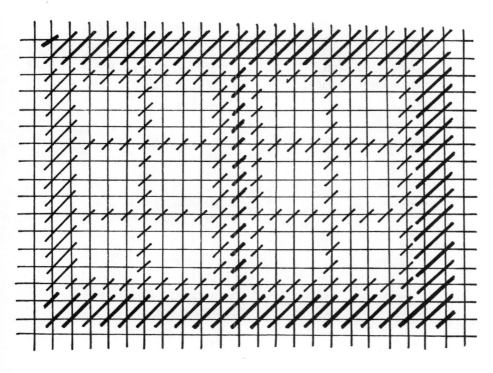

3

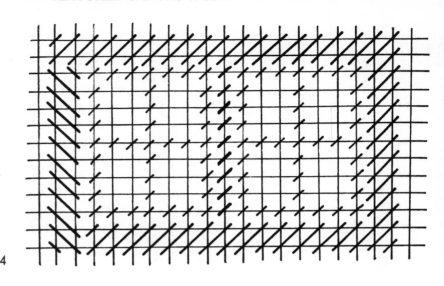

4

4 GARDEN PATH

AREA	STITCH	THREAD/ COLOUR/ NUMBER OF STRANDS
A Path stones	Giant horizontal interlocking gobelin	Overdyed cotton 122/125/170 6 strands
B Grass	Horizontal straight	Tapestry wool 7345
C Background	Random fly	Coton retors mat 2499
D Back bushes	Detached chain	Dansk Fleur HF100 4 strands Stranded cotton 731 4 strands

AREA	STITCH	THREAD/ COLOUR/ NUMBER OF STRANDS
E Berry bushes		
Leaves	Detached twisted chain	Perle coton No. 5 936 2 strands
Flowers	Colonial knot	Stranded cotton 498 6 strands
F Reeds	Straight	Overdyed wool green/brown 2 strands
G Lavender		
Leaves	Detached twisted chain	Medici wool 8407 2 strands
Flowers	Bullion knot (vary the number of twists)	Stranded cotton 3727
H Canberra grass	Cross stitch variation	Coton retors mat 2906
I Alyssum	Colonial knot	Stranded cotton 988 white 4 strands
Weeds between path stones	Coral knot	Medici wool 8414 2 strands

INSTRUCTIONS

Area A (path stones)

As the direction of the path flows from bottom left to top right, so should the stitch pattern. The three colours should be used at random along the path. Each stone is worked entirely in one colour.

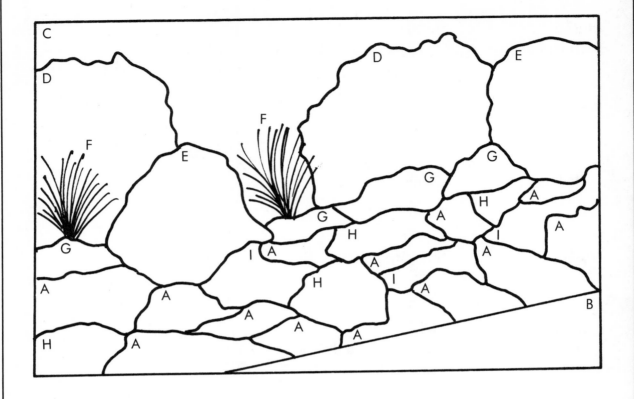

Area B (grass)

To make the grassed area work in relation to the path, make the colour a medium shade and work it in a horizontal stitch.

Area C (background)

To help the front bushes to stand out, this area needs to be a dark colour with little shading.

Area D (back bushes)

If you wish to add flowers, take care that they are not large nor protrude too far or the bushes will appear to come forward. Work the stitches in an upward direction and fan them out towards the edges.

Area E (berry bushes)

For the leaves, stitch downwards and fan them out towards the bottom edge. Stitch the flowers in groups as well as singly.

Area F (reeds)

Stagger the length of the straight stitches, building them up at the base.

Area G (lavender)

Stitch from the base upwards to give the impression of layers, but only use two strands of Medici, or the area will be built up too much in front of the berry bushes.

Area H (Canberra grass)

Build up the area so that they stand out, by varying the size of the cross stitches — and remember to keep the top cross stitch in the same direction.

Area I (alyssum)

Make these areas prominent by stitching the green first and then the white.

Weeds between path stones

To help define and form the edges of the path stones, work coral knots; use a fine thread as they represent weeds.

5 WISHING WELL

AREA	STITCH	THREAD/ COLOUR/ NUMBER OF STRANDS
A Pillars (front)	Double padded cashmere	Overdyed cotton 122 6 strands
B Pillars (back)	Random cashmere	Overdyed cotton 122 6 strands
C Well (front)	Random cashmere	Overdyed cotton 122 6 strands
D Well (top)	Straight	Overdyed cotton 122 6 strands
E Roof	Slanted gobelin	Stranded cotton 3777 6 strands
F Eaves	Interlocking gobelin	Stranded cotton 3021 6 strands
G Wood slats	Straight	Overdyed cotton 170 6 strands
H Sky	Milanese	Stranded cotton 3325 6 strands
I Path	Double stitch variation	Dansk Fleur HF 113 4 strands

AREA	STITCH	THREAD/ COLOUR/ NUMBER OF STRANDS
J Tree trunk	Interlocking gobelin	Overdyed wool shades of brown 2 strands
K Tree canopy	Random fly	Overdyed wool shades of green
L Shrub (right)	Detached twisted chain	Crewel wool 296 3 strands
	Detached twisted chain	Combine in the needle Crewel wool 1 strand of 296, and Perle coton No. 5 1 strand of 319
M Shrub (left)	Buttonhole rings	Overdyed mohair green
N Front plant	Colonial and French knots	Combine in the needle Medici wool 3 strands of 8422, and Perle coton No. 5 1 strand of 730
O Well (inside)	Random cashmere	Stranded cotton 840 6 strands
Wheel Optional	Buttonhole worked over a rubber washer or small curtain ring	Overdyed cotton 6 strands

INSTRUCTIONS

Area A (front pillars)

To bring these pillars forward, pad the base with a double layer of stitches.

Area B (back pillars)

To accentuate the front pillars, stitch the back ones without padding.

Area C (front of well)

Work various sizes of cashmere stitch to fill the area.

Area D (well top)

As you work around the top it will be necessary to adjust the stitching, with some stitches sharing the same hole at the centre to give evenly spaced stitches around the outer edge. Work straight stitches between the top and front of the well to give a neat edging.

Area E (roof)

Follow the angle of the roof with the stitches, filling between the lines.

Area F (eaves)

Work the entire area in a dark shade.

Area G (wood slats)

For the look of ageing wood, use overdyed cotton. Strip the cotton to ensure it lies flat over the previous stitches and lay the straight stitches at an angle to give clean, neat wood slats.

Area H (sky)

Take care when stitching the sky and move the roof slats slightly to allow the sky stitching to go under the stitches.

Area I (path)

As the right side of the path is higher than the left, work a stitch pattern that will flow in that direction. Paths normally have a matt surface, so use a corresponding thread.

Area J (tree trunk)

This is a very small area, so choose a stitch that has a weak pattern.

Area K (tree canopy)

If you are not using an overdyed thread, remember to scatter the dark and middle shade patches over the canopy and have the majority of light stitches at the outer edges.

Area L (right shrub)

This area was stitched with both a dull and shiny thread in the needle at the same time to give depth to the shrub.

Area M (left shrub)

For a heavily textured area, work multiple buttonhole

rings. I worked the rings around my finger, which makes them large enough to then curl on themselves when finished. Stitch the curled rings onto the canvas until the area is filled.

Area N (front plant)

Two types of thread were used in the one needle and then stitched with two types of knots.

Area O (inside of well)

Fill the area with cashmere stitch to represent stones, but use a dark shade.

Wheel

The covered wheel is optional. With a long thread, cover the rubber washer with buttonhole stitch. When completely covered, turn the buttonhole stitch so that the ridge formed is on the inside edge of the washer.

Wheel spokes

Cut a long length of the same thread that covered the rubber washer. Starting at the inside edge of the washer, take the thread directly across to the other side and back to the start, and, working from one side to the other, wrap the thread around these two threads. This makes one spoke. Very carefully take the threaded needle through the wrapping to the centre of the wrapped thread; now take the thread across to the inside edge of the washer and back to the other side of the washer, at right angles to the first spoke. Wrap your thread around to form another spoke.

6 COLUMN

AREA	STITCH	THREAD/ COLOUR/ NUMBER OF STRANDS
A Column Padding	Interlocking gobelin	Overdyed cotton 187 6 strands Extra canvas and rolled pelum are also required
B Sky	Twill	Stranded cotton 3756 6 strands
C Wall Padding Brick	Padded random cashmere Padded random cashmere	Cotton retors mat Overdyed cotton 187 6 strands
D Step	Random cashmere	Overdyed cotton 170
E Landings	Horizontal interlocking gobelin	Overdyed cotton 187/170 6 strands
F Path	Giant horizontal interlocking gobelin	Overdyed cotton 187 6 strands
G Column base Padding	Straight	Overdyed cotton 187 6 strands Rolled pelum is also required

AREA	STITCH	THREAD/ COLOUR/ NUMBER OF STRANDS
H Shrub	Random fly	Tapestry wool 7355 Zig knitting wool green/gold Dansk Fleur HF 29
I Shrub		
Leaves	Detached twisted chain	Coton retors mat 2648/2522
Flowers	Pistil knot (worked in groups of 3)	Stranded cotton 745 4 strands
J Annuals		
Leaves	Bullion knot	Overdyed cotton 142 6 strands
Flowers	Bullion knot	Stranded cotton 902 6 strands
K Spiked plant	Wrapped straight	Perle coton No. 5 936
L Annuals		
Leaves	Colonial knots	Crewel wool 296 2 strands
Flowers	Colonial and French knots	Stranded cotton 347/3328/2712 6 strands
M Climber (optional)	Wrapped threads	Overdyed wool shades of green
Leaves	Buttonhole on a knot	Overdyed wool shades of green
Flowers	Buttonhole on a knot	Stranded cotton 819 6 strands

INSTRUCTIONS

Area A (column)

Since the column is in the foreground and I wanted it to appear to be of marble or a smooth stone, it was necessary for it to be both prominent and in a flat stitch. To keep the smooth texture and give a three-dimensional effect, I stitched an extra piece of canvas and appliquéd it to the base. Work the column in the following way.

1. When the design has been transferred to canvas, count the number of canvas threads, across and down, in the column area and make a note of them. As the extra piece of canvas for the column will be raised, this needs to be larger than the size of the column, so add four threads to the number across.

2. Cut a piece of canvas, the same mesh count as your main canvas, 18 cm x 10 cm (7¼ in x 4 in).

3. On the extra piece of canvas, count and mark the number of canvas threads across and down for the column. This small piece of canvas should be worked in a frame as interlocking gobelin stitch distorts the canvas.

4. Stitch the marked area with interlocking gobelin in the chosen thread.

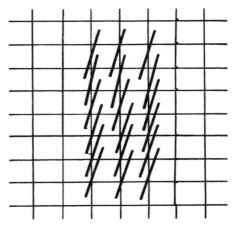

5. Starting from the outside edges and leaving one bare thread around the stitched area, carefully remove all the surrounding canvas threads.

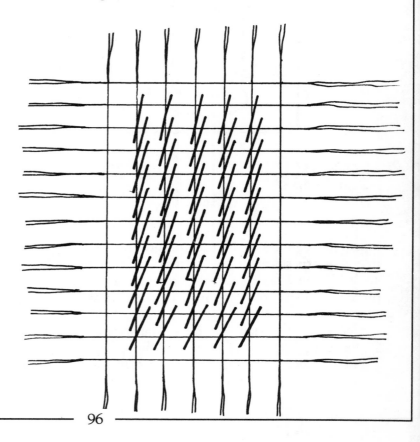

6. The left side of the extra piece will be attached first to the main canvas.
7. Working on the main canvas along the marked line, bring all the individual threads of the extra piece of canvas through the holes of the main canvas with a needle or very fine crochet hook.
8. Make sure the extra piece of canvas is butted up to the main canvas, then anchor the loose threads at the back of the canvas with machine cotton, using back stitches approximately 2 cm (1 in) from the column edge.
9. Secure the extra canvas in place by stitching over the bare canvas threads at its edge and going through to the back of the main canvas, using the same thread and stitch as for the column.
10. Cut a piece of pelum or wadding 5 cm x 12 cm (2 in x 5 in).
11. Roll the pelum lengthways and place under the extra piece of canvas.
12. Take the loose threads on the right side of the extra piece through to the back using either a needle or fine crochet hook.
13. Anchor the loose threads in place as for the other side following step 8.
14. Stitch down the right side of the column following step 9.
15. Stitch the top and bottom edges following step 8 and 9.

Area B (sky)

This is a small area, so the stitch chosen is small and it flows in the same direction as the steps.

Area C (walls)

The stitches for the wall were padded to give the effect of sandstone. The stitch direction was changed to make the column appear to be on a corner.

Area D (step risers)

Usually risers are in shadow, so a dark shade was chosen. With canvas work it is very hard to achieve a true angle line at the top of stitches, I find it easier to divide the step risers into areas and stitch these separately, then lay a stripped thread across the top of the stitches to neaten the edge.

Area E (landings)

A small horizontal stitch was used with a dark shade thread at the corners (next to the wall) and under the stepped areas to help give the effect of a level surface.

Area F (path)

As this area is the foreground, a larger horizontal stitch was used and the stitch pattern flows towards the steps.

Area G (column base)

Work the padded base of the column as follows.

1. Roll a small piece of pelum or wadding approximately 1.5 cm x 1 cm (¾ in x ½ in) and anchor it in place at the bottom of the column, overstitching it with machine cotton.
2. Using the same thread as for the column, carefully straight stitch over the pelum, taking the stitch over the last row of the column stitches. Make sure the thread is lying perfectly flat as you stitch, and adjust the stitches as you work around. The base will have to be top stitched twice to achieve good coverage.

Area H (shrub)

Roughly stitch over the area with tapestry wool to give a padding. Then with Zig wool fill the area, but allow the tapestry wool to show through. Some of the shrub's new growth is red, so I have included a scattering of burgundy stitches.

Area I (shrub)

Scatter the dark shade throughout the area, then fill with the light shade. For the flowers, rather than use single knots I have used pistil knots worked in groups of three. Visually, odd numbers look much better than even.

Area J (annuals)

Working bullion knots in the green overdyed cotton helps give the effect of ageing leaves.

Area K (spiked plant)

I have used wrapped straight stitches in a shiny thread here to add depth, as normal straight stitches would have blended with the background stitching.

Area L (annuals)

French knots were used in this area as this is a small stitch that gives texture and allows changes of colour in a small area.

Area M (climber)

Placing a climber up the column is optional, but the column will look very stark on its own. The climber is worked by using simple wrapped detached threads, with additional leaves and flowers in buttonhole on a knot.

7 RED WINDOW

AREA	STITCH	THREAD/ COLOUR/ NUMBER OF STRANDS
A Window		
A1 Frame	Slanted gobelin	Stranded cotton 349 9 strands
A2 Pane	Giant vertical interlocking gobelin	Stranded cotton 413 6 strands
A3 Side	Slanted gobelin	Coton retors mat 415
A3 Ledge	Slanted gobelin	Coton retors mat 415
B Cement render	Interlocking gobelin	Stranded cotton 415/318 or Overdyed cotton 173 6 strands
C Wall	Random cashmere	Stranded cotton 415/318/317 413/3799 or Overdyed cotton 172 6 strands

AREA	STITCH	THREAD/ COLOUR/ NUMBER OF STRANDS
D Plant pot	Slanted gobelin and continental	Coton retors mat 2922
E Leaves	Buttonhole on a knot	Coton retors mat 2986
F Flowers	Buttonhole on a knot	Perle coton No. 5 666

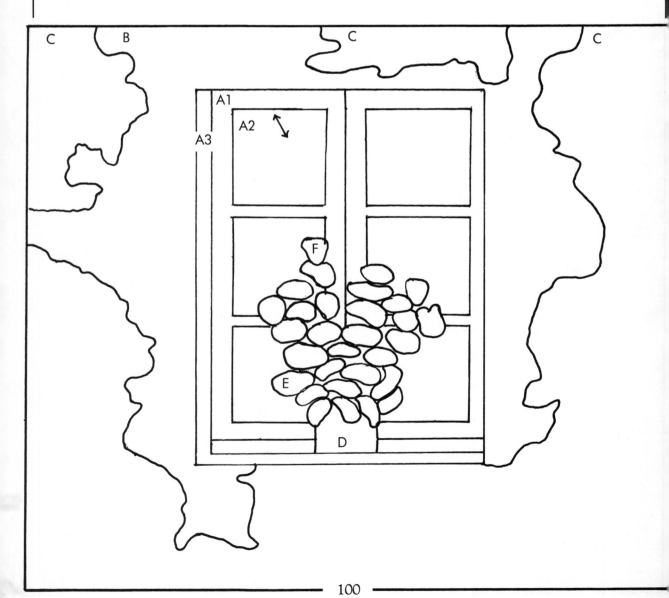

INSTRUCTIONS

Area A (window frame/pane/side/ledge)

Follow the stitch chart below, stitching in the direction of the lines and over the same number of canvas threads. Work the window frame first, using nine strands of cotton (do not forget to strip them). For the panes, stitch in the same direction as the window frame.

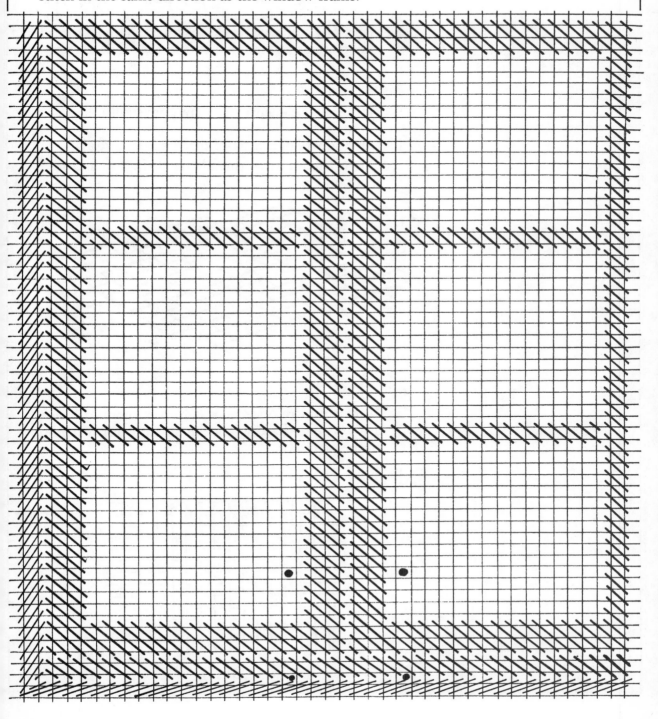

Area B (cement render)

To get the effect of a smooth surface, work with small stitches and scatter the different shades of thread throughout the area.

Area C (wall)

This is an area where you may wish to change the stitches. Vary the sizes and shapes of the stitches for the effect of a stone wall and use either overdyed thread or combinations of stranded cotton for shade changes.

Area D (plant pot)

Work the three-dimensional plant pot as follows.

1. Cut a square of canvas 15 threads x 15 threads.
2. Count three canvas threads from the top and fold them under.

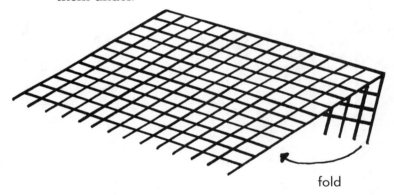

fold

3. With coton retors mat, stitch over the fold, using a row of interlocking gobelin stitch to form the lip of the plant pot.

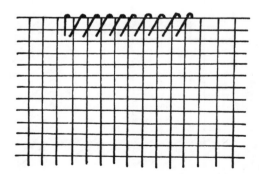

4. Work over nine threads and six rows in continental stitch under the lip.

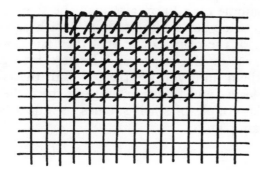

5. Cut away the excess canvas, leaving three canvas threads around the stitching.
6. Fold under two canvas threads on the bottom edge so that there is one bare canvas thread showing.
7. Fold under two canvas threads on both sides. You will now have a small square of stitched canvas with one bare canvas thread showing on three sides.

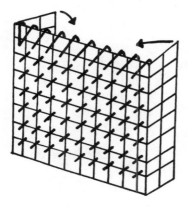

8. Place the piece of canvas on the window at the position marked on the chart on page 101. The canvas should curve out slightly from the picture.
9. Using continental stitch, work down each side over the bare canvas thread, going through to the back of the main canvas. Then carefully stitch across the base, ensuring that the canvas maintains its curve. As you work, make sure that the base stitching butts up to the windowsill ledge but does not go over it.

Areas E and F (leaves and flowers)

Make 20 leaves in coton retors mat and 11 flowers using perle coton. Follow the instructions given on page 67 for buttonhole on a knot, although the shapes may be varied to suit your interpretation. Attach three leaves to the lip of the plant pot so that they hang over, then pin the rest of the leaves and flowers into position, moving them until you are pleased with the effect. So that the leaves and flowers stand out from the canvas, use only a couple of small stitches to attach one edge to the main picture.

8 PICKET FENCE

AREA	STITCH	THREAD/ COLOUR/ NUMBER OF STRANDS
A Fence	Vertical slanted gobelin	Perle coton No. 5 white
B Wall post	Vertical slanted gobelin	Overdyed cotton 171 6 strands
C Wall		
Stones	Random cashmere	Overdyed cotton 171 6 strands
Mortar	Continental	Stranded cotton 3799 6 strands
D Driveway	Giant horizontal interlocking gobelin	Coton retors mat 2233
E Sky	Irregular continental	Stranded cotton 775 6 strands

AREA	STITCH	THREAD/ COLOUR/ NUMBER OF STRANDS
F Back tree	Random fly	Zig knitting wool green
G Conifer	Bullion knot	Coton retors mat 2856
H Front shrub		
Leaves	Detached chain	Coton retors mat 2648/2522 Stranded cotton 501 4 strands
Flowers	Pistil knot	Stranded cotton 745 4 strands
I Tree		
Trunk	Raised stem band	Overdyed wool shades of brown
Leaves	Detached chain in groups of 2	Perle coton No. 5 890/367
Flowers	Colonial knot	Stranded cotton 3608 6 strands
J Iris		
Leaves	Straight	Perle coton No. 5 890
Flowers	Palestrina knot	Overdyed cotton MT 110/2 6 strands
K Annuals		
Leaves	Detached twisted chain	Perle coton No. 5 936
Flowers	Colonial knot	Stranded cotton 340 6 strands

INSTRUCTIONS

Area A (picket fence)

Follow the stitch chart below.

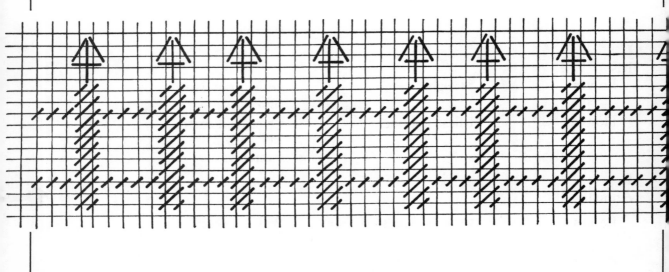

Area B (wall post)

Fill the area with vertical slanted gobelin stitch, making sure the stitch flows in the direction of the arrows. If you are using normal stranded cotton colours, then change to a light shade for the area nearest the driveway.

Area C (wall)

Stitch the stones first, with the stitch flowing in the direction of the arrow, then fill in between with continental stitch in a darker shade.

Area D (driveway)

Make sure that the stitch pattern flows from bottom left to top right.

Area F (back tree)

I used a dark colour Zig wool, but any dark thread would work.

Area G (conifer)

Fill the area with various lengths of bullion knots, working upwards from the base. Make sure that the stitches are interlocked, not worked in rows, for a more natural effect.

Area H (front shrub)

Scatter the dark shade from the base upwards and then fill in with the light shade of coton retors mat. For the flowers, work pistil knots in groups of three, working more at the top of the shrub.

Area I (tree)

By working a raised stem band, the tree trunk stands out from the canvas and this effect can be further enhanced by using overdyed wool. The first step is to fill the area with horizontal straight stitches, then work in rows from bottom to top.

Work the leaves in detached chain stitch, in groups of two. To give the appearance of both mature and new growth, use two shades of thread. Take care with the stitch tension so that the leaves lie on top of the tree trunk.

As with the leaves, be careful that the stitches for the flowers do not sink into the tree trunk. They should be stitched in groups.

Area J (irises)

Work clumps of straight stitches, varying the lengths, and stitch flowers at the top of a few of the stems.

Area K (annuals)

Fill the area with leaves, then scatter the flowers throughout.